D1593050

THE UNKNOWN WAR
WITH RUSSIA

THE UNKNOWN WAR WITH RUSSIA

WILSON'S SIBERIAN INTERVENTION

by

Robert J. Maddox

PRESIDIO PRESS
SAN RAFAEL · CALIFORNIA

THE UNKNOWN WAR WITH RUSSIA:
Wilson's Siberian Intervention
Robert J. Maddox

Copyright © 1977

PRESIDIO PRESS
1114 Irwin Street
San Rafael, California 94901

Library of Congress Catalog Card Number: 76-58761
ISBN: 0-89141-013-9

Printed in the United States of America

For Quinn, Carol and Bourke

Contents

Illustrations

MAPS

Acknowledgements

Members of the staffs in the libraries in which I conducted my research were unfailingly courteous and helpful. The Liberal Arts Central Fund for Research, the Slavic Language and Area Center, and the Institute for the Arts and Humanities at The Pennsylvania State University aided me in preparing the manuscript. I am also grateful for permission to reprint in revised form materials first published as "Woodrow Wilson, the Russian Embassy and Siberian Intervention," *Pacific Historical Review*, XXXVI (November 1967), 435-48.

THE UNKNOWN WAR
WITH RUSSIA

Introduction

On the evening of April 2, 1917, President Woodrow Wilson appeared before a joint session of Congress to request a declaration of war against Imperial Germany. Part way through his message, the president alluded to Russia where a few weeks earlier revolution had toppled the government of Tsar Nicholas II. Referring to these events as "wonderful and heartening things," Wilson announced that the Russian people "in all their naive majesty and might" were now committed to the crusade for peace, justice and freedom which he asked the United States to join. "Here," he proclaimed, "is a fit partner for a league of honor." Within a year, however, Russia had concluded a separate peace with Germany, and a few months later the United States participated in an intervention which the existing government regarded as a hostile invasion.[1]

The Siberian intervention—an event scarcely known outside scholarly circles—can only be understood against the background of American relations with Russia over the years. These relations, official and unofficial, had produced in the United States a set of assumptions about the Russian people and society which greatly influenced American policies. Only the sketchiest account can be offered here, but perhaps even this will help explain why President Wilson sent American troops to Russian soil.

The United States' first minister to Russia was John Quincy Adams, who presented his credentials to Tsar Alexander I in 1809. For the next seventy-five years, the most salient feature of American-Russian relations was the absence of serious conflict. There were disputes to be sure, competing territorial claims on the North American continent, for example—but no clashes over fundamental national interests. Indeed, despite radical differences in political and social structures, there evolved a myth of an historic friendship between the two nations. At times this myth was consciously nourished by American statesmen, as when Secretary of State Henry Seward cited the friendship as one of the reasons why the United States should consummate the Alaskan purchase. Among other things, Seward helped circulate the story that Russia had demonstrated her support of the Union during the Civil War by sending a fleet to visit Northern cities. Actually, the Russians wanted to get their ships out of dangerous waters in case of hostilities with Great Britain, but the story endured.

All this began to change during the last fifteen years of the nineteenth century, a process which continued until the outbreak of World War I. As the United States developed its interests in the Far East, particularly with the acquisition of the Philippines and the enunciation of Open Door principles, the stage was set for rivalry with an expanding Russia, especially in Manchuria and Korea. When Russia and Japan went to war over these regions in 1904, American sentiment favored the Japanese as a plucky little people taking on the Russian bear. The myth of friendship evaporated in the face of real issues.

A growing awareness of domestic conditions in Russia also helped shape American attitudes. Widely publicized accounts of visits to Russia acquainted readers with some of the more deplorable aspects of that society. George Kennan's *Siberia and the Exile System*, first published serially in *The Century* in 1888, then as a book in 1891, was the most notable of these reports. Exposés of Russia proved popular enough to spawn a minor industry over the years. Articles such as "In the Grip of the Tsar," "House of Bondage" and "Stolypin and the New Terror" became commonplace. The literature varied in quality but kept Russia constantly before the eyes of the reading public.

Immigration from Russia and Russia-dominated areas swelled during this period. Some immigrants wished to escape political or religious persecution, others fled poverty or the protracted military service required by the Russian government. Few refugees had any love for the tsarist system; all had some recollection of oppression. In many sections of New York City, for instance, a policeman who resorted to violence could expect to depart amid chants of "Cossack, Cossack."

Specific events influenced public opinion and official relations with Russia. Pogroms against Jews, particularly the Kishinev Massacre of 1903, appalled many Americans. During 1908 and 1909, the so-called Pouren-Rudewitz cases aroused a considerable furor. These two men, avowed revolutionaries, had fled to the United States after committing political offenses against the tsarist government. Under the existing treaty, individuals could not be extradited for political acts. The Russian government sought to skirt this obstacle by demanding the return of Pouren and Rudewitz on the ground that they had committed civil crimes. When an examining commission upheld the Russian request, public pressure against extradition grew to such an extent that Secretary of State Elihu Root overruled the decision. Active in the campaign against extradition were figures such as Jane Addams, Robert M. La Follette, Jacob Riis, George Kennan and Clarence Darrow.

This friction with Russia culminated in what became known as the Passport Question.[2] Ostensibly, the matter concerned the treatment of American Jews travelling in Russia. The United States claimed that all Americans were entitled to equal treatment, while the Russian government insisted that American Jews in Russia must submit to the limitations imposed upon Russian Jews. The real issues lay deeper. Various American groups sought to use the Passport Question as a wedge to ameliorate the dreadful conditions under which Russian Jews were forced to live. To this end they mounted a campaign against the existing commercial treaty as a means of pressuring the Russian government. Skillfully playing upon patriotic sentiment by presenting the Russian position as an affront to American honor, the proabrogationists in December, 1911, forced a reluctant President Taft to inform the Russians that the United States would terminate the treaty. Woodrow Wilson, then a presidential aspirant, was one of the abrogationists' most popular spokesmen.

Although termination of the treaty failed to have any discernible effect on the situation of Russian Jews, the campaign preceding it helped to complete a picture of Russia which had been emerging for some years. In it the tsarist regime was portrayed as utterly cruel and ruthless beneath its ceremonial glitter, totally without concern for the wretched masses upon which it sat. Aggressive in foreign policy, repressive at home, the Russian government seemed perfectly represented by those political cartoons which depicted it as a slavering bear with bloody claws or as a brutish Cossack brandishing knout and smoking pistol.

These negative images of the oppressive government did not extend to the Russian people. Quite the contrary, the Russian masses were, if anything, idealized. Western intellectuals, particularly Americans, have a tendency to invest "primitive" peoples with all kinds of virtues. The Russians were no exception. Time and again one finds the Russian peasant—who made up the bulk of the population—characterized as hardworking and devout, with a spiritual purity uncontaminated by Western materialism and education. Moreover, by pointing to certain local institutions which had survived over the years, a number of writers stressed the idea that the Russian people were democratic by instinct and by custom despite centuries of tsarist despotism.

There are times when popular assumptions differ greatly from those of policy makers. This was not the case with pre-World War I views of Russia. The State Department, at that time a very modest organization, had no Russia specialists. Indeed, it was customary for the department to consult someone from the academic or business community on questions requiring more expertise than the European desk officers could provide. Except for his participation in the abrogation campaign, Woodrow Wilson had shown no particular interest in Russia. Neither he nor his advisers, therefore, had an understanding of the Russian society much more profound than that presented in the popular journals of the day.

To them, Russia was a backward land in which a reactionary government tyrannized a population yearning to be free. This simplistic view meshed easily with the assumption, which Wilson shared with many Americans, that all societies were evolving toward an ideal political and economic structure which the United States, with all its imperfections, had come closest to realizing. When the impact of World War I brought about the March Revolution, the president welcomed it as a confirmation of the evolutionary process. But the Bolshevik seizure of power later that same year appalled him. It heralded a new despotism no less oppressive than the old. Wilson's decision to intervene in Siberia was motivated above all by his desire to help Russia back on the path to liberation as he defined it. The intervention failed because the Russian masses did not respond as he thought they would. His goals were lofty, but they were undermined by the legacy of ignorance he had inherited.

The
Impact
of
War

1

When war engulfed Europe in 1914, leaders on both sides hoped to achieve their goals through decisive military campaigns of relatively short duration. Had that occurred, the course of twentieth-century history would have been quite different no matter who won. Instead, after a brief period of movement, the war became a struggle of attrition, grinding along month after month, year after year, with catastrophic results. A generation of young men was decimated, world empires were mortally wounded, and new forces were unleashed, the significance of which contemporaries could only dimly perceive. The hemorrhages of protracted war caused Germany to take steps which brought the United States into the conflict after two and a half years of neutrality. In Russia, the sufferings of war led to a series of upheavals culminating in the Bolshevik Revolution of November, 1917. These two events, which took place only seven months apart, fused the destinies of both nations from that time until the present.

Most observers exaggerated Russian strength when World War I began. Her command system was inefficient, her equipment mostly obsolete and her armies badly trained, but many people believed that the sheer numbers she could place on the field of battle after full mobilization would compensate for these obvious weaknesses. True, Russia had suffered a military debacle against the Japanese ten years before, but the enormous distances and logistical problems involved in that conflict were unique. While Great Britain and France engaged Germany and Austria-Hungary in the West, the Russian steamroller would win the war on the eastern front. This illusion dissipated quickly.

Although her soldiers at times fought with great courage and individual units acquitted themselves well, Russia's military liabilities soon became obvious: poor leadership at the top, costly rivalries and sheer stupidity among field commanders, and troops who lacked both equipment and proper training. To make matters worse, corruption and inefficiency in the rear guaranteed that armies in the field almost always lacked sufficient food, ammunition and supplies. The combination of all these factors proved disastrous, and numbers counted for little against rapid-firing artillery and machine guns. Russian forces were badly mauled in campaign after botched campaign, with hideous losses and thousands captured.

Nor were Russia's miseries limited to the battlefield, as dreadful as they were. Disaffection at home grew as the months dragged by and the casualty lists lengthened. Shortages of food and fuel became commonplace as the transportation and distribution system collapsed under demands it could not meet. And for what great purpose were the sacrifices being made? To the Russian people the conflict became known as "the tsar's war": they knew little of its goals and cared even less. Morale sagged further as stories spread about pro-German intrigue in court circles—the tsar's wife, who had come from a German principality, was a particular target—and about the baneful influence of the notorious monk, Rasputin.

Some observers predicted as early as 1915 that Russia could not last the year. Like a riderless bicycle, the system wobbled on for a while longer, but its collapse was inevitable. No one masterminded the upheavals of March, 1917; they were spontaneous demonstrations against the war, the deprivations and a regime which appeared wholly unresponsive to the needs of the people. Russian tsarism was not overthrown but rather disintegrated because there was no one left to defend it. When troops in the large cities refused to fire on demonstrators, the Romanov dynasty came to an end.

Meanwhile, in the United States events were rushing to a climax of another sort. When the fighting began, President

Wilson had called upon the American people to be neutral in thought and deed. Although falling somewhat short of this goal in practice, as in the case of making credits available to the Allies, the administration hewed to its neutrality policies until the day the United States declared war. Indeed, it was President Wilson's rigid interpretation of neutral rights, especially those of Americans and American ships on the high seas, which placed the United States and Germany on a collision course. Both the British and Germans infringed upon the rights Wilson claimed, but Germany's use of the submarine (her surface fleet was unequal to Great Britain's) killed Americans, while British violations were mere inconveniences. Wishing to keep the United States out of the conflict, Berlin, during the first half of the war, agreed to limit submarine operations. As the fighting dragged on inconclusively, however, the German high command began arguing that unrestricted submarine warfare was the only way to bring the British and French to their knees. The United States already was supporting these nations economically, the military pointed out, and submarine depredations could choke off this aid before American military forces could become decisive. When the civilian government adopted this strategy (it was made public in late January, 1917), American entry became inevitable.

Historians disagree over Wilson's motives. Granting that the submarine issue was the triggering event, it remains unclear why he insisted so adamantly upon neutral privileges that jeopardized Germany's vital interests. Why did he fail to recognize that the traditional rights of neutrals were obviated by the submarine? Some scholars have maintained that Wilson by instinct and by preference favored the Allies from the start and that his neutral policies reflected his bias. Other historians have emphasized America's economic stake in an Allied victory as a prime cause. Still others have stressed geopolitics, claiming that Wilson recognized that a Europe dominated by Germany and Austria-Hungary posed a threat to America's national security. Whatever the reason, the president made it clear that the United States would participate in the war for purposes far more ambitious than punishing neutrality violations.

Wilson's reading of history had convinced him that wars rarely solved issues, but only bred later conflicts. The victors usually punished their opponents in such a way that the latter devoted themselves to growing sufficiently strong to wrench back what had been taken. If the present conflict were to accomplish lasting results, he concluded, it would have to be fought for goals loftier than the seizure of territories or natural resources. What he sought was a "peace without victory," as he put it, a peace based upon equitable treatment of all nations. He saw it as the only way to break the cycle of recurrent wars.

Another lesson of the past for Wilson was that, while governments often made war upon one another, their citizens invariably yearned for peace. It followed that representative governments would be far less likely to resort to violence. The present war seemed a case in point. Whatever claims each side put forward in its own behalf, it *was* Imperial Germany which had invaded hapless Belgium. Even if a peace without victory could be obtained at war's end, could such a government be trusted in the future? Wilson thought not and subsequently refused to negotiate with the German government as it was then constituted. To the extent that republican governments gained ascendency, he believed, to that extent the cause of peace would be advanced.

The third aspect of Wilson's sense of history was the need for an association of nations. Even under the best of circumstances governments still might blunder into conflict. A formal organization based on the principle of collective security would serve two functions: first, as a mechanism through which disputes could be resolved peaceably; second, as a deterrent to any who would challenge the status quo through force of arms. Wilson's belief in the need for a league of

14

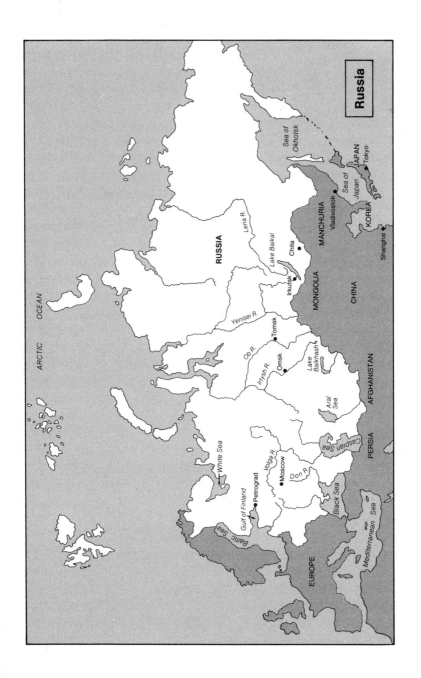

Russia

nations grew strong enough to influence his policies on a number of apparently unrelated issues. This was particularly true regarding Great Britain and France, without whose cooperation no such organization could be forged.

Wilson greeted the March Revolution in Russia as a major step toward achieving the kind of postwar world he envisioned. Not only were the people released from despotism, but Russia under a representative government could take its rightful place among peace-loving nations. The president made sure that the United States was the first to recognize the Provisional Government which had succeeded Tsar Nicholas II and referred to Russia in his war message as a "fit partner for a league of honor." Although the Revolution exerted no perceptible influence on his decision to ask Congress for a declaration of war against Germany, it afforded him an inspiring rationale. Now the European struggle could more easily be depicted as a clash between the forces of democracy and those of reaction and militarism.

The Revolution also boded well for the conduct of the war itself, or so it first appeared. If, as was widely believed, Russia's fighting spirit had been undermined by the tsarist regime's corrupt, wasteful conduct, perhaps it could be regained under democratic leadership. Successes on the eastern front might well turn the tide in the West, where French and British forces were threatened by renewed German drives. Leaders of the Provisional Government—mostly former members of the ineffectual Russian Duma (parliament)— encouraged these hopes; they portrayed themselves as a stable, middle-class group dedicated to a strong war effort. Their periodic declarations to this effect received wide publicity in the United States, stimulating confidence that Russia would become an increasingly significant factor in the war's outcome.

This optimistic view had no basis in fact. In the first place, the Provisional Government's control within Russia was contested from the outset by the soviets (worker's councils) in the large cities. Dominated by socialist parties, though not yet by the Bolsheviks, these organizations exerted an ever greater influence within the armed forces. They were willing to support only a defensive war, not one based on the tsarist war aims endorsed by the Provisional Government. Second, and equally important, the Russian people were heartily sick of the war, no matter under whose auspices it was fought. The rejuvenation of fighting spirit predicted by officials of the Provisional Government was an illusion.

Within weeks the Wilson administration learned how critical the situation in Russia really was.[1] Although information received from regular American representatives in Russia often was inadequate—the ambassador, David R. Francis, was an aging Missouri politican with no previous diplomatic experience—evidence of the Provisional Government's extreme frailty steadily mounted. Loans, which had been denied the tsarist government, were made available to Russia, but any effects they might have other than psychological lay in the future. Besides, the Russian transportation system was in such disrepair that enormous amounts of supplies and equipment already had accumulated at various port cities. A major crisis occurred when the much-heralded Russian summer offensive, after some initial successes, ended disastrously. The tsar's war had become the Provisional Government's war, and the Russian people hated both.

The failure of the offensive unleashed great turmoil in Russia and led to a reorganization of the Provisional Government. Demands for peace discussions based on the formula, "No annexations and no indemnities," reflected the growing influence of the soviets. Earlier pledges to continue the struggle until Allied war goals were attained could not be kept. The precise details of these goals were unknown to the public—they were embodied in a series of secret agreements among the Allies—but it was widely understood that they called for territorial acquisition and the like. Now Russian officials believed the government's very life depended on a

16

restatement of war aims. Seeking desperately to force the issue upon their reluctant partners, they threatened to publish the secret treaties, should their pleas go unanswered.

The facade of Russian-Allied unity threatened to give way at the worst possible moment. French and British armies were barely holding their own on the western front, and the United States as yet had contributed only token forces. If the Russian government collapsed or negotiated a separate peace, the number of German divisions which could be transferred from the eastern front might tip the balance. And yet, Allied leaders reasoned, the enormous losses already sustained prevented them from redefining their war aims. It was an argument heard before and since: to stop short of victory would mean that the sacrifices made thus far had been in vain. The Western Allies, therefore, spurned Russia's requests. Instead, alternating appeals to honor and threats of economic coercion, they tried to convince the Provisional Government to carry on as before.

Events in Russia precipitated a public debate in the United States and confronted Wilson with a painful dilemma. Despite the apprehensions about the Provisional Government he and Secretary of State Robert Lansing had shared for some time, administration press releases continued to speak of it in the most glowing terms. Reports appearing daily in the newspapers now questioned such optimism. More and more voices were raised, in Congress and elsewhere, calling upon the president to disassociate himself from Allied policy. Senator William E. Borah of Idaho became one of Wilson's most vocal critics on this issue. Since Russian armies refused to fight for the spoils of war, said Borah, they should be encouraged to fight in defense of their own revolution. Having no commitment to any secret agreements, the United States should regard itself free to act independently. To do otherwise meant endangering the lives of American soldiers who would have to face reinforced German armies in the West if Russia collapsed. He urged the president to do anything necessary to prevent such a debacle, no matter what the cost to British or French sensibilities.[2]

Wilson himself had great sympathy for the Provisional Government's appeal. The slogan "No annexations and no indemnities," he believed, struck a responsive note with the peoples of the world and should be exploited. He knew as well that Russian leaders looked to the United States as the power most likely to appreciate their difficulties. But what of the Western Allies? The president had to bear in mind their determination to achieve the goals set down in the secret treaties. A unilateral stand aimed at negating these arrangements would sorely damage American relations with France and Great Britain for the duration of the war and then during peace negotiations. This consideration, together with the opportunities it presented for creating a viable world order, had by this time grown paramount in shaping Wilson's diplomacy.

The president already had indicated what his response would be. In June the American journalist, Lincoln Steffens, had returned from Russia bearing a private message from the Provisional Government seeking Wilson's support in revising the war aims. According to Steffens, the president grew "very disturbed" upon reading the request and expressed his great desire to satisfy Russia's demands. In the end, however, he told Steffens, "That I cannot very well do"—this at a time when Wilson confided to his wife his fear that Russia would "soon be in a state of revolution."[3]

Now, in late July, the French requested Wilson to clarify his position on the Provisional Government's threatened exposure of the secret arrangements. After a period of agonizing hesitation, the president elected to maintain solidarity with the Western Allies despite his misgivings. These he set down in a draft reply to the French. He did not see how Russian demands could "wisely be rejected," because world opinion made it imperative that the Allies demonstrate that

18

they fought not for territorial conquest "but for the freedom of the peoples to secure independence. . . . The President hopes," he concluded, "that the issue can be met squarely and candidly." These phrases undoubtedly represented his innermost feelings, just as he had expressed them to Steffens a month earlier. Yet, recognizing their incompatibility with Allied objectives, he filed the draft and refused to support Russia's appeal.[4]

Whatever his sentiments, Wilson's policy toward Russia was indistinguishable from that of the Western Allies. While expressing hopes that the Provisional Government could somehow consolidate its position, they prodded it into continuing a debilitating struggle. Yet the war's unpopularity with Russian soldiers and civilians made these goals contradictory. In addition, the president sought ineffectually to bolster Russian morale through loans, inspirational messages and a gaggle of American missions. Among these were a Red Cross unit, a contingent of railroad experts and the so-called Root mission. Former Secretary of War and State Elihu Root, a seventy-three-year-old conservative lawyer and politician, led a group of business and labor leaders on a month's tour to promote goodwill, as well as to observe conditions. It is doubtful that this mission or any other accomplished anything useful. One labor figure lectured a Russian audience on the value of union labels, while Root himself tried to impress upon Russian officials that they had *better* stay in the war: "No fight, no loans," as he crudely put it.

Allied and American diplomacy during this period raises an interesting historical "if." If France and Great Britain had agreed to revise their war aims or if Wilson had interceded publicly, could the Provisional Government have stayed afloat and avoided the Bolshevik takeover? Russian officials believed, or claimed to believe, that a redefinition of goals would reverse the decline of the armed forces. Even if Germany failed to respond, and it was unlikely that she would have moderated her goals, the war could be better justified as a struggle against German aggression. And the charge of waging an unnecessary war did count heavily against the Provisional Government.

Such faith in the power of rhetoric now seems unwarranted. Since the war had always been defended publicly on the grounds of noble ideals, how much impact could a new variation have had? Officials of the Provisional Government never accurately gauged how war-weary the Russian masses really were. Besides, opponents of the regime would have alleged that revision of the war aims was just a ruse designed to gain support for an imperialist conflict. Actually, in view of the Provisional Government's grave deficiencies in organization and leadership, its chances of surviving a continuation of the war—no matter what its announced goals—must be judged as small. It is certain, however, that Allied and American policies undercut even this possibility.

Conditions in Russia worsened through the summer and fall. Under attack from both left and right, the Provisional Government had no strong base of support among the people. Although Ambassador Francis consistently exaggerated the regime's strength, a great deal of more reliable information flowed into Washington during these months. Pessimistic themselves, Wilson and Lansing nevertheless continued to purvey a version of Russian affairs they did not believe. As late as November 2, Secretary Lansing stated publicly that the Provisional Government, rumors notwithstanding, planned to "organize all Russia's resources in a wholehearted resistance and carry the war through to a victorious conclusion." The statement was pure fiction.[5]

On the night of November 7 armed forces of the Petrograd soviet, now dominated by the Bolsheviks, surrounded the Winter Palace. Inside, members of the Provisional Government met in fruitless sessions, searching for ways to halt the disintegration of their authority. Earlier that day Premier Alexander Kerensky had left Petrograd by automobile, hoping to find loyal troops with which to put down the insurrection.

A few hours after midnight, finding a rear door unprotected, Red Guards entered the palace and arrested the government officials. The coup was relatively bloodless. As in the March Revolution, the regime had been overthrown because there was no one left to defend it.

The Bolshevik coup produced great confusion in Washington. Since several days elapsed before even the first sketchy reports arrived from Ambassador Francis and other Americans on the scene, Wilson and his advisers knew little more than what appeared in the press, that a Bolshevik uprising had seized control of Petrograd, forcing Premier Kerensky to flee the city.

At first there were indications—expressions of hope, actually—that Kerensky himself, with the aid of loyal military units stationed outside Petrograd, might be able to put down the insurrection. Several stories appeared about anti-Bolshevik forces advancing upon the city. When such claims were discredited, numerous Russian "experts" hurried forward to present their views of what would happen next. One theory, advanced from several sources, had it that events in Petrograd were made possible only by that city's unique location and history. Petrograd was not really Russian, it was said, and the Bolsheviks could never succeed in interior population centers such as Moscow.[6] This proposition lost its currency when the Bolsheviks took power in Moscow a short while later.

With little to go on besides rumor and speculation, the Wilson administration refrained from any official announcements. According to a story in the *New York Times*, an entire cabinet meeting on November 9 was given over to a discussion of conditions in Russia. Not surprisingly, the conclusion was that the American government would adopt a wait-and-see policy. Those cabinet members who spoke to reporters after the session maintained at least a facade of optimism. "It was apparent from the expressions of high officials," one reporter noted, "that hope has not been abandoned that Russia would remain in the allied column and yet give assistance to

21

the Entente, Japan, and the United States in winning the war." Whether this view accurately reflected the tenor of the discussions or was designed for public consumption is not clear; no official record of the meeting has been found. Reporters were also told, however, that the American government almost certainly would refuse to continue aid to any regime which sought to take Russia out of the war, a course the Bolsheviks had advocated all along.

That same day, one high official—probably Secretary of State Lansing—offered his own speculations to some members of the press. Perhaps, he suggested, something good would come out of the confusion after all. In response to the Bolshevik insurrection, some Russian "strongman" might emerge to solidify the nation as the Provisional Government had failed to do. Should this occur, there remained a chance that the eastern front could be resuscitated. Although never as sanguine as Lansing about reviving Russia's war effort, President Wilson himself became an advocate of the "strongman" solution. And, as events showed, he was willing to interfere in Russian affairs to achieve that end.[7]

During the first blush of enthusiasm for the March Revolution, Wilson had predicted that the democratic instincts of the Russian people would produce a state capable of sustaining the war against Prussian militarism. When this proved illusory, his concern for Allied-American solidarity prevented him from taking steps which might have helped the Provisional Government secure its position. Now the worst had happened: the Provisional Government had been overthrown by a group dedicated not only to radical social principles which he abhorred but to ending a war he believed must be won in order to create a better world. "I have not lost faith in the Russian outcome by any means," Wilson wrote to a congressman four days after the Bolsheviks took control of Petrograd. He qualified his optimism, however, by predicting that Russia "will no doubt have to go through deep waters" before coming out "upon firm land."[8]

The American Response to Bolshevism

2

In retrospect, the Bolshevik Revolution of November, 1917, stands as one of the most significant events of the twentieth century. But this was not obvious at the time. To Western leaders, including President Wilson, the most important aspect of the coup was its possible effect on the course of the war. Would the Bolsheviks conclude a separate peace with Germany, thereby closing down the eastern front? Or could they be persuaded to resist German encroachments in defense of their own revolution? Perhaps the Bolsheviks themselves would be overthrown and a more "responsible" government would emerge in Russia. The possibilities seemed almost endless, and everyone had his own idea about how to proceed. While Wilson undoubtedly detested bolshevism, at that time his immediate desire to win the war overshadowed ideological considerations which would later seem crucial.

Bolshevik slogans about ending the war were translated into policy as early as November 8. On that date, Lenin called for an international peace conference to end the conflict but warned that his regime meant to remove Russia from the fighting regardless of what other governments might do.[1] If the leaders of the warring powers disregarded this appeal, Lenin proclaimed that they should be overthrown by the peace-loving masses. Shortly thereafter the Bolsheviks notified Germany of their desire to open peace talks and, within a month, formal negotiations began in the town of Brest-Litovsk, German army headquarters in Russia. It was unlikely that any governments would be destroyed because of appeals emanating from Petrograd, but Russia's departure from the war could prove disastrous. Equally dangerous, from Wilson's point of view, was the possibility that Bolshevik initiatives might raise hopes in the United States and elsewhere that an

27

equitable peace could be negotiated with the Central Powers. Having for some time been convinced that the existing German government could not be trusted, the president regarded the notion as a cruel illusion made more treacherous by its appeal to the widespread longing for peace. The need to discredit such hopes became uppermost in his mind.

There were complications. Outright condemnation of the Bolshevik appeal might push them closer to a bilateral settlement with Germany. It would also place the United States in the position of appearing to oppose genuine efforts to stop the carnage. Furthermore, since much of the rhetoric in the proclamation resembled Wilson's earlier statement, he would be repudiating his own lofty sentiments. In Wilson's view, the wrong people had appropriated perfectly desirable programs for their own ends. The problem, therefore, was to recapture the initiative for himself and to channel the longing for peace into a proper set of goals.

On November 12, Wilson first indicated his strategy, while making a speech in Buffalo, New York, to a convention of the American Federation of Labor. Toward the end of an address devoted almost entirely to the need for speeding up the war effort, Wilson mentioned those who thought it possible to negotiate with the militarists in Germany and Austria-Hungary. He sympathized with such people, he said, but he could not abide their "stupidity." Those Americans who harbored such beliefs impeded the war effort and were as wrongheaded as the "idle dreamers" of Russia. He, the president, wanted peace as badly as anyone, but "he knew how to achieve it while they did not."[2]

Wilson's fears were exacerbated several weeks later when a spokesman for the German government stated publicly that the Bolshevik proposals seemed generally acceptable. Rather than believing the Germans were sincerely trying to end the war on equitable terms, the president assumed that they were trying to split the Allies and undermine their morale through duplicity. Still, if such tactics destroyed the will to prosecute the war to a successful conclusion, the president believed that everything done so far would have been in vain. On December 4, in a message which accompanied his request to Congress for a declaration of war against the Austro-Hungarian Empire, Wilson responded. His address developed more fully the themes he had touched upon in his earlier speech to the A.F.of L.

Wilson first justified the war as a crusade against "this intolerable Thing" which he defined as a "menace of combined intrigue and force which we now see so clearly as the German power, a Thing without conscience or honor or capacity for covenanted peace." Only when Allied and American power had smashed that "Thing" and the German people "have spokesmen whose word we can believe" could a lasting peace be achieved.

There daily grew more audible, Wilson continued, the "voices of humanity" which demanded that the war not end in "vindictive action of any kind." Unfortunately, evil men sought to pervert these sentiments for their own ends. Citing the so-called Petrograd formula of "no annexations, no contributions, no punitive indemnities," the president warned that the "masters of German intrigue" were conniving to "lead the people of Russia astray." The thing to do, of course, was not to abandon such goals but to see that they were in fact realized— and to ignore the seductive words of those who wanted a "premature peace" before "autocracy had been taught its final and convincing lesson."

Whether the president meant to imply that the Bolshevik leaders themselves were under German influence or merely that they had been tricked by the Germans is not clear, but there is no doubt as to his conclusion. No lasting peace could be negotiated with the existing governments of the Central Powers. Therefore, Wilson declared, "Our present and immediate task is to win the war, and nothing shall turn us aside from it until it is accomplished."[3]

It is against this background that the relevance of Wilson's famous Fourteen Points to the situation in Russia can best be understood.[4] Ever since the November Revolution, the president had been besieged by advice on policy. Some voices, domestic and foreign, pleaded that the United States join some form of armed intervention to topple the Bolsheviks. Others argued that the Bolsheviks were in control of European Russia, like it or not, and that the best course for the United States was to work with and try to influence Soviet leaders. Some added that the Bolsheviks would fight the Germans if supported and encouraged. Because thus far the administration had made few official pronouncements about relations with Russia, those portions of the message concerning this subject were anxiously read for indications of what the president's attitude was likely to be.

There is no question that Soviet peace appeals precipitated Wilson's statement of war aims. He had considered such a move the previous summer but had held off, not wishing to provoke friction with Great Britain and France over the obvious conflict between a peace without victory and the goals embodied in the Allies' secret treaties. Now, however, he was prepared to risk their displeasure in order to prevent the Bolsheviks from exploiting the widespread desire for an end to the war.

In his introductory remarks, Wilson pointed to the Russo-German peace talks as indicative of the futility of negotiating with the Central Powers. Under the mistaken impression that the parleys had broken off because of extreme German demands, he scorned those who had been so naive as to hope for anything else. Preliminary statements of German goals probably had come from liberal elements, he said, and reflected a genuine desire for fair settlements. Once it came to actual negotiations, however, it was the "military masters" of Germany who called the tune. Their demands made it clear beyond doubt that Germany meant to seize all the territory it could. Equating the statements of the liberals with the true feelings of the German people, Wilson dramatized the contrast between this yen for peace and the ruthlessness of the military. His conclusion was simple: the war must be pushed to a victorious conclusion before lasting arrangements could be made.

In his discussion of the Brest-Litovsk talks, Wilson alluded several times to the conduct of the Bolshevik government and its representatives. He praised their insistence upon open negotiations, their goal of a peace without annexations or indemnities and their refusal to continue discussions in the face of Germany's imperialist demands. Then, in the sixth of his Fourteen Points, the president referred to the obligations of other nations to succor Russia "under institutions of her own choosing." The manner in which these obligations were met would be the "acid test" of goodwill in the months to come.

Wilson's references to Russia created a stir. Advocates of accommodation with the Bolsheviks sensed in his generous comments about the Bolsheviks a retreat from the administration's previous unwillingness to recognize the Soviet government. Surely such statements about the Bolsheviks must mean that he had at last come around to the view that the United States should try to work with them rather than ignore them. Others, of contrary opinion, immediately denied that the president meant to indicate anything of the sort. The controversy over what the Fourteen Points portended for Russia has since engaged scholars almost as heatedly as it did contemporaries.

People at the time, as well as more recent observers, may have read too much into Wilson's comments as they pertain to Russia. In context the president's praise for the Bolshevik negotiators and their program merely provided the backdrop against which he enlarged upon his theme that no just peace could be arranged with the present rulers of the Central Powers. In his earlier A.F.of L. speech, he had referred to those Russians who sought peace with Germany as "idle dreamers." Now, believing the discussions had foundered, he praised both their program and their conduct. To have criticized the Bolsheviks on grounds of bad faith or mistaken tactics would have suggested that their stated goals might have had some chance of success in more capable hands. This was precisely the notion that the president wished to dispel.

To some observers, Wilson's subsequent unwillingness to recognize the Bolshevik government and his decision to intervene in Russia constituted a betrayal of the Fourteen Points. However, a close reading of the document suggests that his references to the Soviets were less generous than they first appeared. For instance, throughout his message German negotiators are designated as "representatives of the Central Powers," while their Bolshevik counterparts are invariably referred to merely as "Russian representatives." Not once did the president indicate that they actually represented a legitimate Russian government. Perhaps this reflects no more than a stylistic preference, but to use this construction without exception may indicate that the president meant to cover himself technically.

In any event, Wilson's statements about Russia in Point Six are ambiguous. Although those who advocated cooperation with the Bolsheviks thought his reference to Russia "under institutions of her own choosing" indicated a retreat from the administration's previous refusal to deal with them officially, it is patently clear that the president did not regard the Soviet government as representing the will of the Russian people. To him it was a regime which had seized power forcibly during a time of deep internal stress. The fact that the Bolsheviks had dissolved the Constituent Assembly, convened by the Provisional Government to create a permanent, representative structure for Russia, confirmed this belief.

It is probable, therefore, that Wilson concealed his true feelings about the Bolsheviks in his Fourteen Points Message in order to defend his position that the war must be prosecuted until the Central Powers were defeated. And he had another reason. Although mistaken in thinking that the Russo-

German talks had already broken off (which did not happen until a few weeks later), the president refrained from openly antagonizing the Bolsheviks for fear it would "drive them into the arms of Germany," an expression commonly used at the time. His closest adviser, "Colonel" E. M. House, had warned him against this from the beginning. In this respect as well, the war's importance overshadowed all other considerations.

Decisions made behind the scenes strongly suggest that President Wilson opposed the Bolsheviks from the outset and never had the slightest intention of reaching an accommodation with them. One of the first of such decisions concerned the status of the Russian embassy in Washington and the large sums of money at its disposal. Although it would be incorrect to attribute too much foresight to the president about such a fluid situation, his actions in this case point to intentions which official pronouncements did not reveal.

One of the first actions of the Provisional Government had been to dispatch a diplomatic mission to replace that of the tsarist regime. This mission, headed by an urbane scholar-businessman named Boris Bakhmetev, served also as the Provisional Government's procurement agency.* Between March and November, 1917, the United States advanced 325 million dollars in credits to the Provisional Government, of which almost $188 million was used prior to the Bolshevik Revolution. The embassy in addition controlled funds and assets realized through the sale of Russian bonds before the tsarist government's collapse.[5] When the Bolsheviks took power, of course, it meant that the ambassador and his staff represented a deposed government.

On November 11, Ambassador Bakhmetev announced that he would not accept the authority of the Bolshevik regime.

---

*Apparently wishing to show his contempt for autocracy, President Wilson refused to receive the departing tsarist ambassador, George Bakhmetev. When asked by a reporter whether he and Boris were related, Bakhmetev replied that their relationship was about the same "as Booker T. Washington's to George."[6]

He admitted that the Soviets appeared to have overthrown the Provisional Government but viewed this as a temporary aberration made possible by the strains of war. Asserting his confidence in the democratic "spirit" of the Russian people, he predicted that the Bolsheviks would be replaced by a liberal, representative system. For the present, Bakhmetev maintained, the embassy would continue to function while awaiting the rise of a legal successor.[7]

The ambassador's statement coincided with—and probably was prompted by—the administration's assessment of the situation. President Wilson's "wait and see" policy was based partly on the hope that the Bolsheviks represented only a "phase," and that they too would pass from the scene. In keeping with this attitude, the State Department announced that events had not changed the status of Bakhmetev and the embassy. Since the Soviet regime had not appointed the ambassador, the department held, he had no obligation to abide by its dictates.[8] Aside from representing an item of diplomatic *curiosa*—continuing to recognize the ambassador accredited by a deposed government—the arrangement attracted little attention at first.

In fact, the administration's position seemed sensible. There was no way of knowing whether the Bolsheviks would survive, and Bakhmetev could resume his procurement functions without interruption should they go under. The ability of any Russian government to resume active military campaigning had to be discounted, but subsequent leaders might be able to consolidate defensive lines against the Central Powers. Even a stabilized eastern front would require German and Austrian units otherwise free for duty in the West.

But the embassy could serve another purpose as well, and American policy makers were aware of it from the outset. The funds and assets formerly under Bakhmetev's control could be used to influence events in Russia according to the administration's aims. Within a week of the November Revolution, Bakhmetev was informed that henceforth all his transactions must have the approval of the United States government. In a series of meetings between the ambassador and representatives of the State and Treasury Departments, procedures were worked out which effectively placed the embassy's resources at the disposal of the administration. Bakhmetev was nominally the Russian ambassador but in fact was a disbursing agent for the United States government.[9]

Bakhmetev supplied a limited amount of nonmilitary goods to Russia during the first few months after the revolution, some of it to areas under Bolshevik control. The administration decided that, as long as the Soviet government had failed to reach an accord with Germany, the Russian people should not think that America had "abandoned" them in their hour of need. This comported with overall Allied policy which deemed a "mere armistice" preferable to driving the Bolsheviks into German arms.[10] But wartime exigencies alone dictated such restraint. Administration officials simultaneously discussed using embassy funds to nourish an anti-Bolshevik movement being organized in southern Russia. Although nothing came of this particular venture, it became clear that the embassy would be a kind of dummy corporation, a cover through which the technically neutral administration could discreetly assist anti-Communists.

Wilson's decision to aid opponents of the Soviet regime also belied his public statements about Russia. Within weeks of the revolution it was reported that a General A. M. Kaledin and several other high-ranking Russian officers were organizing anti-Communist forces in southern Russia. Information received in Washington indicated that these men were able, energetic and commanded great loyalty among their followers. It was also learned that Great Britain and France were willing to aid the Kaledin movement any way they could and sought American cooperation.

On December 2, Colonel House, who was representing the president at an Allied conference in Paris, cabled his views. He thought that the Allies' proposal was fraught with danger "because it encourages internal disturbances without our having in mind any definite program or any force to back up a program." Yet, he went on, it was very likely that the anti-Bolshevik movement would "go to pieces" if not aided and encouraged. Although he made no commitments, House suggested to the French and British that the United States would be willing to advance them funds for aiding Kaledin. That way, he concluded, the United States would "not appear in the transaction openly," and if it turned out to be a mistake this nation "would occupy a more favorable position" than the Allies.[11]

Secretary of State Lansing also wished to support Kaledin. In a memorandum to the president written a week after House's cable, Lansing stated his conviction that the Bolsheviks "are determined to prevent Russia from taking further part in the war." The longer they stayed in power, "the more will authority in Russia be disorganized and the more will the armies disintegrate." Russia's departure from the war, he believed, would prolong the conflict for two or three years. If, on the other hand, Bolshevik domination were "broken," the Russian armies might be reorganized and "become an important factor in the war by next spring or summer." According to the secretary, "The hope of a stable Russian Government lies for the present in a military dictatorship backed by loyal disciplined troops." To encourage this prospect, Lansing suggested sending word to Kaledin that the United States had no intention of treating with the Bolsheviks but stood ready to recognize a government strong enough "to restore order" and "to carry out in good faith Russia's international engagements."[12]

According to Lansing's desk diary, he and the president met almost every day on this issue for a week.[13] The result was Wilson's decision to implement House's proposal that the United States indirectly finance Kaledin through the British and French. Lansing drafted a cable to this effect for the American financial representative in London, stressing the need for secrecy. This was necessary, he wrote, because the administration could not legally loan money to a regime it had not recognized and "because of the attitude which it seems advisable to take with the Petrograd authorities." Wilson returned the draft to Lansing with the notation, "This has my entire approval."[14]

Thus the administration's announced policy of nonintervention in Russian affairs was for tactical purposes only, designed to prevent the Bolsheviks from accommodating the Germans with whom they were negotiating. The quick collapse of the Kaledin movement (the general himself committed suicide) should not obscure the president's willingness to take sides in Russia's domestic strife. He would be willing to do so in the future, albeit under more secure circumstances, for the Kaledin fiasco had left him far more cautious about extending aid to anti-Bolshevik groups until he became convinced that they had at least a reasonable chance of success.

It is against this background that Wilson's view on military intervention in Russia must be understood. Demands for some sort of intervention—usually assumed to be through the Siberian port of Vladivostok—were raised almost as soon as the Bolsheviks seized power. They came at various times from Great Britain, France and Japan, and from Americans within and outside of the administration. The expressed goals of such a step varied as well: to help reconstitute the eastern front (with or without Bolshevik cooperation); to prevent German penetration of Siberia; or, more modestly, to protect the vast supplies of materials which had accumulated in Vladivostok.

The information Wilson received about conditions in Russia was, if possible, even more confusing. Some reports indicated that the Bolsheviks were prepared to resist Germany, if assisted by the Allies; others denied this. Stories circulated that Lenin and Trotsky were German agents, plotting for the Central Powers. From Siberia came a welter of conflicting messages on subjects such as the progress of anti-Bolshevik groups in forming governments, the attitude of Siberian Bolsheviks toward intervention, and the status of German and Austrian prisoners-of-war who, according to some reports, were organized, armed and ready to seize key cities in Siberia.

With such confusion, it is small wonder that Wilson refused to countenance intervention during the first months of 1918. There were other reasons as well. The French and British, after toying with a number of schemes, agreed that the Japanese should undertake the project in behalf of the Allies. At best, they argued, the eastern front might be reopened. Even if this failed, however, the fact that Japan was taking a more active role in the war would strike a psychological blow at the Germans. The Japanese government indicated its willingness to invade Siberia if the United States approved. On a few occasions, Tokyo hinted that it might act even without such approval but failed to do so.

Wilson opposed the scheme. In the first place, his military advisers had assured him that a Japanese expedition had no chance of penetrating as far west as the military lines, thousands of miles from Vladivostok. Indeed, there was little reason to believe the Japanese themselves were interested in moving much beyond eastern Siberia, regardless of French and British aspirations. There was concern within the administration as to the real Japanese intentions. Once they had moved into Siberia, would they ever leave? Or would they use the opportunity to expand the Japanese empire? Even the British had to admit this possibility but argued that the risk was worth taking. Wilson reached the opposite conclusion.*

The specific problems entailed by a Japanese expedition aside, the president fundamentally objected to intervention by anyone. If forces were sent in, he argued over and over,

---

*He modified his position briefly in February-March, 1918. While still unwilling to approve a Japanese expedition, he had prepared a message indicating the administration would no longer object to it. He did so, apparently, because he was under the impression at that time that the Japanese were prepared to act unilaterally. House and others argued vigorously against the change, whereupon Wilson abandoned it.[15]

would not the Russians regard it as an invasion? In fact, he thought intervention would strengthen the Bolsheviks rather than weaken them, for it would enable them to pose as defenders of the nation's sovereignty against intruding foreigners. The president's sensitivity about this prospect is understandable. His unhappy experience with Mexico—to which he alluded when discussing Russia—had taught him that interference could be treacherous business, no matter how loftily motivated.* That the French and British failed to appreciate this consideration Wilson attributed to their desperation over conditions on the western front.

By late March, 1918, demands for intervention grew more vehement. By this time, the Soviets had signed and ratified a separate peace with Germany embodied in what became known as the Treaty of Brest-Litovsk. The treaty permitted the Germans to accelerate troop movements from east to west, already underway, and guaranteed their access to resources located in the Russian territories they occupied. Equally ominous for the Allies was Germany's launching a spring offensive in the West against exhausted British and French armies. Wilson acknowledged and appreciated the situation but repeated his objections to intervention. Nothing he had seen so far, the president wrote on one occasion, could "answer the question I have put to . . . [those] who argue in favor of intervention by Japan, namely, what is it to effect and how will it be efficacious in effecting it?"[16]

The president's refusal to countenance a Japanese expedition did not mean he had abandoned hope of influencing events in Russia. Far from it. On March 14, for instance, he told the British ambassador that he was "endeavoring to find a way both to reconcile [the] American people to the need for intervention and to allay Russian fears of it." What he had in

---

*In 1916, Wilson had sent a military expedition into Mexico in pursuit of Pancho Villa, who had crossed the border and committed atrocities against American citizens. To his dismay, Wilson found that practically all Mexicans, even Villa's enemies, resented the American presence.

THE UNKNOWN WAR WITH RUSSIA

mind was a joint Japanese-American expedition which would assist sympathetic Russians in the task of "reorganization." The difficulty, as always for Wilson, lay in finding a means to make intervention palatable to the Russian masses. Several days earlier he had addressed an inspirational message to the Russian people (not to the Soviet government), emphasizing America's desire to be of help to them. "It is most unlikely," the ambassador concluded in his report to London, "that he [Wilson] will take it [intervention] up officially unless the message produces a sympathetic reply from some body of opinion in Russia." The message elicited no such response.[17]

Unable to discern any ground swell of Russian support for intervention, Wilson turned to the idea of assisting one or another of the anti-Bolshevik "governments" which had sprung up in eastern and southern Russia. None of these had more than the flimsiest claims to legitimacy, but perhaps with outside help the most viable one could become the basis for what Wilson had in mind, that is, the "body of opinion" which would request Allied intervention in behalf of all "responsible" Russians.

Throughout April and May, Wilson urged Secretary of State Lansing and others to secure as much reliable information as possible about these anti-Bolshevik groups (or Whites, as they became known). "I would very much value a memorandum containing *all* that we know about these several *nuclei* of self-governing authority that seem to be springing up in Siberia," Wilson wrote to Lansing. "It would afford me a great deal of satisfaction to get behind the most nearly representative of them if it can indeed draw leadership and control to itself.[18] (Italics in original.) In May the president asked Lansing to assess what General Gregori Semenov was "accomplishing" in Siberia to determine whether "there is any legitimate way in which we can assist."*[19]

---

*Semenov was a Cossack leader who attempted to create an independent government in Siberia. He later fell under Japanese influence, becoming little more than a puppet.

Some scholars have emphasized morality as an important factor in Wilson's reluctance to intervene, saying that direct interference in the affairs of a sovereign state ran counter to his strong belief in self-determination. But this misses the point that to Wilson the "real" Russia was that of the March Revolution: liberal, democratic and dedicated to winning the war against the Central Powers. There was no doubt in his mind that the vast majority of Russians shared his views. The Bolsheviks were the usurpers, whether or not they were German agents, and it was they who prevented Russia from exercising self-determination. An intervention designed to reconstitute the "real" Russia, therefore, was perfectly justifiable. And though Wilson had reservations about the motives of his allies, he had none about his own.

The president summed up his feelings about intervention most cogently in a discussion with a British intelligence officer on May 29. "He remarked that he would go as far as intervening against the wishes of the Russian people—knowing that it was eventually for their own good—providing that he thought the scheme had any practical chance of success." Those suggested so far, however, "were in his opinion impracticable, and would have the opposite effect to that desired." When the Britisher asked whether that meant that nothing at all should be done, Wilson replied: "No, we must watch the situation carefully and sympathetically, and be ready to move whenever the right time arrives." In short, Wilson's objections to intervention had been pragmatic ones all along and would vanish when the "right time" arrived.[20]

The
Decision
to
Intervene

3

Developments in June and early July, 1918, led President Wilson at last to approve intervention in Siberia. He did so with great apprehension, mindful of the risks such a course would entail. His apprehension was justified. The plan he devised scarcely resembled what France and Great Britain had advocated for the past six months and, it soon became clear, was not what Japan had in mind either. Moreover, public and congressional attitudes posed a problem which influenced not only policies directly relating to Russia but also Wilson's other programs, such as the league of nations he wished to establish at the war's end. The president tried to counteract these factors, at times deviously, but with only partial success.

One of the new developments affecting Wilson's thinking was the success of the German spring offensive. Launched a few days after ratification of the Brest-Litovsk Treaty in mid-March, this drive achieved important advances and almost split the French and British armies (at one point preparations were made for the evacuation of Paris). The fact that German divisions formerly stationed on the Russian front had taken part in the assault and that more were in transit dramatized the pleas of the British and French that some action be taken in the East. The Germans already enjoyed a numerical superiority in the West, it was argued, and if their reinforcements arrived faster than American units bolstered the Allies, all might be lost.[1]

Wilson never deviated from his belief that foreign troops alone could not reconstitute the eastern front. His military advisers were unanimous on that point, citing the enormous distances and logistical problems involved. Still, if an intervention were mounted which the Germans perceived as an indirect threat, perhaps they would retain the troops which could tip the balance in the West. Were not the stakes involved worth the risk? And finally, however dubious the prospects, Wilson did not want to appear callous to his wartime partners. Years later, former Secretary of War Newton D. Baker recalled a conversation he had had with Wilson at the time: "I convinced him that it [intervention] was unwise, but he told me that he felt obliged to do it anyhow because the British and French were pressing it on his attention so hard and he had refused so many of their requests that they were beginning to feel that he was not a good associate, much less a good ally."[2]

Another consideration was the attitude of anti-Bolshevik groups in Russia. Previously, especially before ratification of the Brest-Litovsk Treaty, it had been argued that intervention might push the Bolsheviks into the arms of Germany, as well as strengthen them because of the opposition non-Bolsheviks might feel toward outside interference. But now a new interpretation was voiced in a number of quarters. According to this view, the Bolsheviks had made peace with Germany, so that aspect of the situation no longer mattered. Domestically, the Soviets had strengthened their grip on the areas they controlled, and the radical nature of their doctrines had become all too apparent. Where did this leave the anti-Bolsheviks? Whatever their persuasion, they could be expected to turn to any source which promised liberation from Communist rule. If the Allies failed to intervene, might the anti-Bolsheviks not turn to Germany for support? It is impossible to determine how much this thesis influenced Wilson's thinking, but the "phase" interpretation of Soviet domination was becoming increasingly untenable.

By all means the most significant new development in Russia involved the Czechoslovak Legion. Originally composed of Czechs and Slovaks living in Russia who wished to fight the Central Powers, this organization had been augmented by their kinsmen from the Austro-Hungarian army who had either surrendered or had been taken prisoner. The legion had performed well on the battlefield, most notably in the ill-fated Russian spring offensive of 1917. The goal of the Czechs was to obtain commitments from the Allies that an independent Czechoslovakian nation would be carved out of the Austro-Hungarian empire at the war's end.

The Brest-Litovsk Treaty left the Czechs stranded. They wished to go on contributing to the Allied cause but could no longer do so on the Russian front. Since the Germans and Austro-Hungarians obviously would not permit them through their lines, the only alternative appeared to be the route east along the Trans-Siberian railway to Vladivostok. Once there, they could be transported by sea to the West, provided the Allies could find the necessary ships. Placing themselves under overall command of the French, who promised to provide the necessary vessels, the Czechs also began negotiating with the Soviet government for safe passage across Siberia.

The Bolsheviks reluctantly granted the Czechs right of transit. They had no wish to anger the Germans and Austro-Hungarians by collaborating with what amounted to an Allied army, but neither did they like the idea of having that army of about 65,000 troops on Russian soil. The Czechs were required to turn over all arms except those necessary for self-defense, before beginning their long journey. Almost immediately charges of bad faith on both sides jeopardized the agreement. When local Communist groups delayed or impeded their trains, the Czechs believed they were acting on orders from higher up. When the Bolsheviks learned that individual soldiers had smuggled aboard unauthorized arms, they in turn accused the Czech leaders of perfidy. By late May, after a number of incidents and with the legion strung out along the railway, a small war erupted all across Siberia.

The outbreak of fighting between Czechs and Bolsheviks seemed a boon to advocates of intervention, particularly the British and French. To the standard arguments of the past six

47

months they now added two more: that a failure to aid the Czechs would constitute betrayal of loyal allies and that the Legion itself, backed by a strong intervention, could become the wedge for a reconstituted eastern front. The Czechs' predicament also struck President Wilson as opportune. Upon learning of it, he envisioned the "shadow of a plan that may be worked along with Japanese assistance."[3]

For some weeks the president had been considering sending a purely economic commission into Siberia, one headed by a person of international stature like Herbert Hoover. Sending the commission would be a gesture of support for non-Bolsheviks in Siberia, but there is evidence that the president had more in mind. Perhaps the goodwill engendered by such a move would create enthusiasm among "responsible" Russians for broader intervention in the future. Or, if the Bolsheviks interfered with the group, let alone physically endangered it, an appeal for outside assistance from someone of Hoover's reputation might provide a similar opening. Now, however, the plight of the Czechs created an entirely new situation. They were the "cousins" of the Russians, as Wilson himself put it, and intervention in their behalf would be less likely to alienate the Russian masses.[4]

It must be emphasized that Wilson had by no means converted to the Franco-British point of view about the likelihood of reestablishing the Russian front directly. That, he continued to believe, was out of the question. What he seems to have had in mind was this: the Czech Legion was a disciplined, reliable body needing only sufficient arms to become the most potent army in Siberia. Already astride the railway to the interior, it could serve as a strategically located cadre for anti-Communist movements, those "nuclei" of which Wilson and Lansing so often spoke. The most viable of these, or combination of them, would be protected and given time to organize economically, politically and, above all, militarily. If, as Wilson firmly believed, the overwhelming majority of Russians were anti-Bolshevik, the new government would

48

attract thousands of volunteers. Looking even further ahead, it might defeat the Soviet regime and bring Russia back into the Allied camp. Indirectly, therefore, Wilson hoped to reconstitute the eastern front, as did Great Britain and France, but he thought it could be done only by the Russians themselves, not by foreigners.

The president's analysis of the situation determined the kind of intervention he proposed. Viewing the United States as the only party without ulterior motives, Wilson tried to assure that this nation alone determined the scope and nature of the operation. Thus, although the expedition would be composed of equal numbers of Japanese and American troops (and he later agreed to Japan's exercising military command), the economic commission following behind it would be exclusively American.* Coupling this with public pronouncements and his own continued leadership, Wilson hoped to restrain the Japanese from using intervention for their own purposes.

Wilson also intended to exclude Great Britain and France from participation, for two reasons. First, given their oft-stated intentions of reopening the eastern front, he was afraid the Russians would feel "used" rather than aided. Second, Wilson had information (false, it turned out) that the British and French already had made agreements regarding spheres of influence in postwar Russia. "He knows what the French and English want," Colonel House noted in his diary, "therefore he thinks it essential to work out a plan with the Japanese."[5] Whatever their intentions, the Japanese alone probably could be pried out of Siberia if Great Britain and France joined the United States in pressuring them. But the United States would be isolated if the two European powers had regional schemes of their own.

---

*Wilson proposed that 7,000 troops be sent from each nation, which happened to be the number of soldiers the United States had available in the Far East at that time (they were stationed in the Philippines). The Japanese had far more, of course, but the president tried to get them to agree to strict limitations.

Ideally, from Wilson's standpoint, the intervention would take place as follows: a modest force, far too small to be interpreted by the Russians as any kind of invasion, would protect Vladivostok and a portion of the Trans-Siberian railway, thereby permitting the Czechs to consolidate in the interior. They in turn would act as a midwife to the birth of a powerful anti-Bolshevik movement. Establishing only defensive positions, the intervening troops would be ostensibly neutral, but in fact they would be maintaining a pipeline to nourish anti-Bolshevik armies.

The way in which the president implemented his plan confirms this interpretation. On July 6, the final decision to intervene was made at a White House meeting.[6] Two days later, Secretary Lansing summoned the Japanese ambassador, Viscount Kikujiro Ishii, to inform him of Wilson's terms. Although he could not commit his government to the plan, Ishii felt that Tokyo would find it satisfactory. The limitation on troops would be an impediment, but the ambassador said that the matter probably could be worked out. Ishii, like the Americans, underestimated the furor this restriction would cause in his own government.

The British and French were not informed of Wilson's decision. Some scholars have attributed this to a "regrettable oversight," but the evidence indicates otherwise. Only hours after Lansing had met with Ishii, Wilson talked with Lord Reading, the British ambassador. Reading's report of the conversation permits little doubt that Wilson consciously and deliberately withheld his plans from the Western Allies until he had reached an accord with the Japanese.

Wilson was quite explicit with the ambassador, telling him about the conference held two days earlier and naming those who had attended. He furthermore informed Reading that Lansing had met with the Japanese ambassador to discuss intervention. Yet the president omitted the crucial points that he had decided to act and that Lansing's talk with Ishii was to secure Japanese cooperation in the venture. Indeed, the overall tenor of Wilson's remarks—he spoke at length about the undesirability of diverting anyone or anything from the western front—led Reading to precisely the wrong conclusion. He reported to his government that the president's views had not changed and that the United States was no closer to intervention than before.[7]

Wilson's plans began coming apart almost at once. It occurred to Lansing that in all likelihood the Japanese would inform the others regardless of what the United States did. Quickly revealing his apprehensions to the president, Lansing asked for and received permission to convey the decision to the Allies on the ground that they would be even more perturbed to learn of the proposed action from Japan, in which case "we may be embarrassed." Lansing said that in his opinion it would be better to be candid with them "now that the Japanese government has had time to consider our proposed program"—in other words, after the fact.[8]

The British and French *were* offended by Wilson's failure to inform them of his decision.[9] And they had no intention of being excluded from the operation. The British ordered a battalion stationed in Hong Kong to proceed to Vladivostok, and the French simply declared that henceforth the Czech Legion was an integral part of the French army. Lesser members of the Allied and Associated Powers sent "show the flag" detachments. Now the intervention had become something other than Wilson intended, though it still fell a long way short of the scale advocated by the Allies. The latter consoled themselves with the hope that the expedition would have to be augmented at a later date.

The Japanese also proved uncooperative. On July 24, more than two weeks after Lansing handed Ishii the American proposal, Japan's reply was received in Washington.[10] Wilson found it most disturbing. In the first place, Japan refused to accept the troop limit of 7,000 he had suggested. It proposed instead to send in one division (approximately 12,000 men) initially, and more would follow if Tokyo found it necessary.

51

Equally ominous, from the president's point of view, were references to Japan's "special position" in Siberia and her desire to work "in harmony" with the Allies (the United States was an Associated Power, but not technically one of the Allies). What this meant, in fact, was that the Japanese intended to pursue their own goals in Siberia, unencumbered by the restrictions Wilson had proposed. He had expressed reservations about their motives in the past; their reply confirmed his worst fears.*

A week before receiving the Japanese message, Wilson had prepared on his own typewriter an aide-mémoire explaining and justifying the intervention.[11] This was circulated to the Allied embassies on July 17, and paraphrased portions of it were released to the press early in August. The document is important, not because it revealed Wilson's thinking on the matter (some of the passages he wrote were untrue or irrelevant) but because of the purposes he intended it to serve. Japan's unwillingness to accept his terms rendered it even more significant.

Wilson began the aide-mémoire by affirming America's unshakable determination to win the war. So long as the situation on the western front remained "critical," Wilson continued, the United States would not divert its forces from that theater. After "repeated and very searching reconsiderations of the whole situation in Russia," moreover, the United States had concluded that "military intervention" would damage Russia rather than help her and contribute nothing to the defeat of Germany. By "military intervention" he meant the large forces requested by France and Great Britain.

"Military action is admissible," the president maintained, "only to help the Czecho-Slovaks consolidate their forces and get into successful cooperation with their Slavic kinsmen and

*The Japanese subsequently modified their terms a bit, because of American pressures. As George F. Kennan, in *The Decision to Intervene*, has pointed out, this could scarcely have reassured Wilson as to their real motives.

to steady any efforts at self-government or self-defense in which the Russians themselves may be willing to accept assistance." Should anyone else develop plans inconsistent with these limited objectives, he warned, the United States would feel "obliged to withdraw" its forces from the venture. He furthermore asked that all the powers associated with the project give "the most public and solemn" assurances that they did not contemplate "any interference of any kind with the political sovereignty of Russia, any intervention in her internal affairs, or any impairment of her territorial integrity either now or hereafter." He concluded by stating that it was his intention to send in a commission of "merchants, agricultural experts, labor advisers" and representatives of charitable organizations at the "earliest opportunity."

The aide-mémoire contained several messages intended for several audiences. First, it was meant to assure the Russians that intervention would not constitute an attempt to "use" them, either during the war or after, and to express support for "efforts at self-government or self-defense." The latter phrase, of course, referred to anti-Bolshevik "efforts," for these were the groups the Czechs were expected to help. In addition, Wilson also was informing Great Britain, France and Japan that the United States would not be a party to any imperialistic schemes already agreed on or devised later. By calling upon those powers to issue pledges of noninterference in Russian affairs, the president sought to bind them to his own program of working through indigenous Russian forces.*

Those portions of the aide-mémoire released to the press were designed to allay domestic criticism. The public version went beyond the original in identifying those who threatened

*It should be pointed out here that the aide-mémoire also referred to small landings at Murmansk and Archangel in northern Russia. Wilson had agreed to these for the purpose of guarding stores against capture by the Central Powers. Although France and Great Britain had some notions about linking these forces with those in Siberia, Wilson and Lansing entertained no such ideas and regarded them as completely separate operations.[12]

the Czechs as "the armed Austrian and German prisoners of war who are attacking them." There had been clashes between Czechs and prisoners-of-war on a small scale, but the latter were either those who had gone over to the Bolsheviks or were simply trying to make their way back home from Siberia. However, Wilson gave the false impression that the prisoners-of-war were actual elements of German and Austrian armies. By failing even to mention the Bolsheviks, Wilson defined the operation entirely in terms of the war effort. People who might have objected strenuously to American participation, however indirect, in a Russian civil war would find it difficult to criticize an effort to rescue loyal allies from destruction by the Central Powers.

Ingeniously worded though it was, the aide-mémoire was a unilateral statement which the parties to whom it was addressed had no obligation to accept. Japan's reply to Wilson's original proposal of July 6 showed the limitations of moral suasion. Indeed, the Japanese response so discouraged him that he seriously contemplated backing out altogether. "The President is fretted with the Japanese attitude," Colonel House noted in his diary. "As a matter of fact, they have never wanted to intervene on an altruistic basis such as the President has insisted upon . . . [he] sent rather a peremptory note to our ambassador in Tokyo, telling him that unless they would agree to intervene on our terms, there would be no intervention at all with our consent."[13]

Still, there were the Czechs to consider, and Wilson probably convinced himself that the Japanese could be restrained in the long run, especially if the alternative were to have them go in alone. The aide-mémoire could yet serve two purposes. Since none of the powers repudiated it openly, they could be said to have assented to its terms. The onus of violating an agreement, therefore, could be placed on any nation which tried to go beyond Wilson's program. And if this failed to deter them, the United States could at any time withdraw from the expedition in keeping with the president's announced threat to do so.

Having decided to go ahead in spite of his dismay over Japan's behavior, President Wilson set the operation in motion. Even before Lansing had conveyed the American proposal to the Japanese on July 6, government officials had begun estimating the amounts of supplies and equipment which could be delivered to the Czechs on short notice. Secretary of War Newton D. Baker informed Wilson on July 2 that the War Department had more than "13,000 rifles and one million rounds of ammunition" which could be dispatched to Vladivostok at once. It should be made clear that by this time there was no talk of "rescuing" the Czechs; the goal was to permit them to consolidate in the Siberian interior, with the intervening forces acting as a rear guard on the route to Vladivostok.

Although its role will be treated at length in a following chapter, it is appropriate to mention briefly the Russian embassy's contribution to the procurement process. In addition to supervising the release of supplies already located in Vladivostok, Ambassador Bakhmetev began sending materials from the United States on transports previously chartered by the Provisional Government and still under the embassy's control. "Frankly I do not know what Boris Bakhmetev represents," one State Department official noted in a memorandum. "We conveniently say he is representing *Russia*."[14] Whatever he represented, Bakhmetev was a key figure at this stage: within weeks he was able to request shipping licenses for a consignment of 100,000 rifles.[15] The president directed all American agencies to lend their full cooperation without which little could be moved because of the wartime transportation shortages. The War Department, the War Industries Board and other organizations assisted Bakhmetev in providing the equipment—some of it destined for the Czechs, the rest for the White armies they were helping to spawn.

As for military personnel, the War Department on August 3 notified the Philippine command to send the Twenty-seventh and Thirty-first Infantry Regiments and supporting units to Vladivostok as soon as shipping could be obtained. As both regiments were under strength, they were to be reinforced by men from the Eighth Division at Camp Fremont in California. The two regiments arrived at Vladivostok by mid-August; the reinforcements landed two weeks later.

On the advice of Secretary Baker, Wilson appointed Maj. Gen. William S. Graves to head the American Expeditionary Force in Siberia. Graves, a professional soldier with impeccable credentials, received his orders in a most unusual fashion. Having only recently been given command of the Eighth Division at Camp Fremont, Graves was notified on August 2 to proceed at once to Kansas City. There, at the railway station, he met with Secretary Baker for instructions. According to Graves's recollection, their conversation was brief. Baker handed the general a copy of Wilson's July 17th aide-mémoire and then said: "This contains the policy of the United States in Russia which you are to follow. Watch your step; you will be walking on eggs loaded with dynamite. God bless you and good-bye."[16] Secretary Baker, events would show, was guilty of understatement.

Americans
In
Siberia

4

When American troops walked down the gangplanks at Vladivostok, they entered a world in which chaos was the normal state of affairs. The city teemed with thousands of military and civilian personnel from more than a dozen nations, and no one was in charge. In order to safeguard their rear, the Czechs had recently overthrown the local administration, which they suspected of being too friendly toward the Bolsheviks. Adding to the disorder were uncounted tons of supplies and equipment strewn about the city and the surrounding hillsides. Mouldering bales of cotton lay next to uncrated automobiles and machinery of all kinds. Vladivostok was a microcosm of Siberia: the old order had broken down and nothing stable had arisen to take its place. "The fact that we were not troubled by custom inspectors and quarantine officials," General Graves wrote later, "was my first initiation into a country without a government."[1]

Had Graves been a more imaginative man—or a less disciplined soldier—he would have been totally bewildered. The only orders he had received, President Wilson's aide-mémoire handed him by Secretary Baker, were vague, to say the least. For instance, what was meant by the phrase, "to steady any efforts at self-government or self-defense in which the Russians themselves may be willing to accept assistance"? Since this obviously referred to groups other than the Bolsheviks, did it not authorize American forces to assist actively the various White factions? Some officials, most notably in the State Department, wanted the general to interpret his instructions that way. He refused. To Graves, the operative part of the aide-mémoire was the president's request that all the powers join together in assuring the Russian people that "none of the governments uniting in action . . . contemplates

61

any interference of any kind with the political sovereignty of Russia, any intervention in her internal affairs, or any impairment of her territorial integrity." Insofar as he was able, Graves hewed to this position the entire time he was in Siberia and thereby incurred the anger of practically everyone else involved.

In actuality, of course, the very nature of the mission precluded real neutrality, as Graves himself understood. Regardless of how American troops behaved in specific instances—and the general made every effort to see that they treated all factions impartially—they functioned as enemies of the Bolsheviks. After all, the rail system they guarded was the lifeline between Vladivostok and the Czech-White armies in the interior. In addition, the activities of America's "partners" in the intervention (over which Graves had no control) further ensured that United States troops would effectively take sides in the Russian civil war, no matter how correct and technically neutral their conduct. This dilemma confronted Graves almost as soon as he assumed command.

Because of the configuration of the border between Manchuria and Russia, the Trans-Siberian railway runs over three hundred miles north from Vladivostok to the town of Khabarovsk before turning west to the interior. Shortly before Graves's arrival, elements of the Twenty-seventh Infantry Regiment, commanded by Col. Henry D. Styer, had joined the Japanese in a sweep along this section of the line and had pushed some miles west of Khabarovsk. The initiative for this operation had come from the Japanese, who had informed Styer that some 15,000 "enemy" troops in that region were preparing a drive upon Vladivostok. The enemy, according to the Japanese, was a combined force of German and Austrian prisoners-of-war and Bolsheviks; its mission was to capture the enormous stores located in the port city.

Graves initially approved American participation in the so-called Ussuri campaign (the Ussuri River ran parallel to the line in this area) because he believed it comported with his

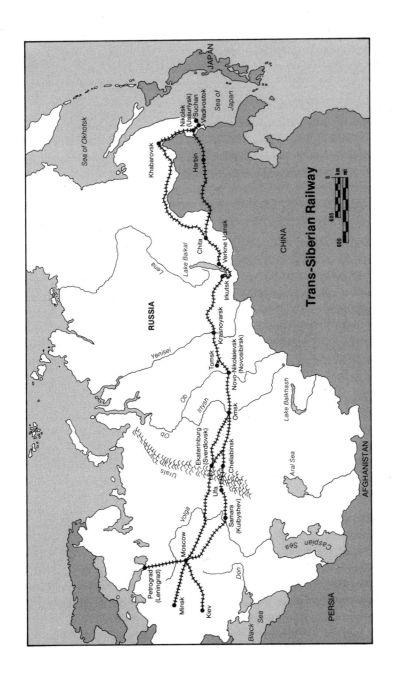

Trans-Siberian Railway

orders to keep the railroad open and to protect military supplies. Subsequent intelligence reports and his own inspection
tour soon convinced him that the Japanese had misrepresented the situation. No enemy force had been poised to attack
Vladivostok, but the Japanese had used this fiction to conduct,
with American help, an operation against all elements they
regarded as unfriendly. From this and other incidents, the
general concluded that the Japanese (as well as the British
and French) were prone to identify all but the most reactionary groups in Russia as Bolshevik collaborators with the German and Austrian prisoners-of-war.

The general ordered American units which had moved
west of Khabarovsk to return to the city. Thereafter, he
refused to permit the use of American troops unless he
believed that the mission fell within the scope of his instructions. Although President Wilson had agreed that the Japanese would exercise overall military command, he had transmitted no such orders to Graves. When the Japanese
commander raised this issue with Graves, the latter replied
that American forces would remain independent until he
received formal notification to the contrary. The instructions
never came and the Japanese, for reasons of their own, did
not press the matter.

Despite Graves's determination to avoid American participation in a repetition of the Ussuri campaign, a second task
undertaken by United States troops soon after they landed
impressed upon him the impossibility of true neutrality.
Approximately seventy-five miles east of Vladivostok lay the
Suchan mines, chief source of coal for the rail lines in eastern
Siberia. The mines had all but ceased operations because of
the factional struggles among Bolsheviks, former supporters
of the tsar and groups in between. In order to get the mines
back into production Graves agreed to participate in an expedition to restore order in the region. Led by an American
officer, a mixed force consisting of one company each of
American, Japanese and Chinese troops was dispatched.

Conditions there were to plague General Graves for the rest of his stay in Siberia.

Graves sent his chief of staff, Colonel O. P. Robinson, with the first troops. Robinson's job was essentially diplomatic. First he had to convince the miners that the coal they produced would benefit other Russians, not merely the foreign military groups. Then he had to persuade them to permit the return of managers and administrators whose protsarist sympathies had alienated the miners in the first place. Finally, Robinson was to prevent retaliation by the returning supervisors against dissident miners and make sure that the occupying troops were not used to suppress political activities.

Although Robinson somehow negotiated working arrangements among the parties, he had barely returned to Vladivostok when reports began arriving that the agreements were being violated by all sides. Graves immediately took steps to correct the situation, but he could influence only the symptoms, not causes. He could do nothing to alter the fact that the coal produced was destined for the use by a rail system which supplied materials to anti-Bolshevik armies. Sabotage and guerrilla attacks became commonplace in the Suchan area, as did retaliatory raids by the occupying forces. Impartiality in this context, as in the intervention as a whole, was a sham.

Except for those units stationed along the route to Khabarovsk and in the Suchan region, the A.E.F. remained in Vladivostok for the first few months after its arrival. For his command headquarters Graves rented a building formerly owned by Germans, and for his men he took over barracks previously used by the tsarist government. The latter, Graves recalled, were perfectly satisfactory "with the exception of bathing facilities which did not exist."[2] For the time being then, American troops busied themselves in the routine tasks of occupation duty: patrolling and guard details, drill and inspections. In their free time they wrote letters, explored the city, visited the countless vodka shops and sought out available women.

Meanwhile, to the west, the original Czech-Bolshevik clash had developed into a full-blown civil war. By late summer Czech units had seized control of the Trans-Siberian railway from the Volga to Vladivostok. They helped create friendly governments in the cities they captured and cooperated with the burgeoning White military forces. The Czechs defeated the Bolsheviks in almost every engagement and conducted offensive operations as much as two hundred miles from the rail line. They were, for the moment, the dominant force in Siberia.

August and September were crucial months for the outcome of intervention. If, as John Bradley has pointed out, Japanese and American units had moved west and allowed the Czechs to consolidate with the Whites along the Volga front, they might have inflicted decisive defeats upon Bolshevik armies.[3] The French and British urged such movements, but to no avail. Japan made it clear that her interests were restricted to eastern Siberia. Wilson, still convinced that efforts to reopen the eastern front were doomed, replied that the United States would make no effort to sustain the Czechs west of the Urals and recommended that they pull back from the Volga.

Therefore, despite their successes in the field, the Czechs were in a precarious situation. They were spread far too thinly, and morale plummeted when it became known there would be no massive shift west by the intervening forces. The Czechs had been led to believe they were going to fight against the Central Powers and that they would be assisted by their Japanese, American and European allies.* Instead, they were fighting Russians and felt betrayed when reinforcements never arrived. From this point on, the legion deteriorated as an effective military force.

---

*With communications between governments and their representatives in the field already poor, junior military and consular officials added to the confusion by consistently exceeding their authority. In this case, French and American representatives badly misled the Czechs about what assistance they could expect.

These were critical weeks for anti-Bolshevik Russians as well. Although one refers to Whites as opposed to Reds, the former is little more than an expression of convenience. Ranging in political sentiments from Monarchists to Social Revolutionaries, they never achieved real unity. A plethora of governments existed, none with more than the flimsiest claim to legitimacy and none which attracted the loyalties of large numbers of Russians. Individuals and factions within each group jockeyed for position, argued interminably and failed to coalesce into functioning organizations. Nor did any single leader emerge around whom the anti-Bolsheviks could rally.

Russia's allies bore a full share of blame for the instability. Graves's abstinence from interfering in political affairs was not matched by his counterparts. On the contrary, British and French military missions constantly schemed. Lacking troops, they dealt in promises of money and supplies. Both pursued the goal of a second front almost until the armistice, and both sought the destruction of Bolshevism. But frequently they acted at cross purposes, backed different contenders and suspected (with good reason) one another's motives. The Japanese, who cared nothing at all about a second front, actively worked against anti-Bolshevik unity because they believed a weak and divided Russia would provide a better opportunity for Japanese expansion in Siberia. They sponsored divisive figures such as Gregorii Semenov and Ivan Kalmikov, Cossack leaders who in fact were little more than bandit chieftains.

The basic weaknesses of the Czech-White position became obvious during September. By that time the Bolsheviks had obtained from the Germans an agreement which freed Red troops to engage their enemies on the Volga front. During the month Red armies scored a series of victories which pushed the Czechs and. Whites eastward. Poorly disciplined and inexperienced, the Bolsheviks were unable to exploit their successes. Given their condition, the fact that they won at all was ominous.

The Red advance was halted when Czech units returning from Vladivostok joined their comrades. But now most Czech soldiers merely wanted to go home. They would defend themselves if attacked and agreed (reluctantly) to go into reserve, but no longer would they bear the brunt of the fighting. White armies, nourished by supplies sent from Vladivostok, had grown steadily and at least numerically were capable of taking over. The problem was that no central authority existed which could give them leadership and direction. An "all-Russian" government, with its seat at Omsk, was formed during October to meet this need. But it failed dismally and was as paralyzed by factionalism as its predecessors.

What happened next is unclear. By early November American representatives in Omsk were reporting rumors of a coup against the Directory, as the newly formed government was called. On the night of November 17, an uprising overthrew the moribund regime. Admiral A. V. Kolchak, formerly of the tsar's navy and more recently minister of war under the Directory, declared himself "The Supreme Ruler of all the Russias." What has intrigued and baffled scholars ever since is whether the British played a direct role in Kolchak's coup. The chief of the British military mission in Siberia and in Omsk at the time was Maj. Gen. Sir Alfred Knox, known to be as partial to Kolchak as he was disgusted with the Directory.[4] And the fact that the Twenty-fifth Middlesex Battalion, the only British force in Siberia, arrived in Omsk a few days before the coup strikes some as more than coincidental. The battalion did not take part in the uprising but was on duty in various parts of the city and probably helped prevent resistance against Kolchak's followers. There are indications that the British, at least at Knox's level, participated in the plot.

Kolchak's seizure of power initiated a new phase in the Siberian operation. The admiral was a man of unquestioned courage and integrity, having served with distinction in both the Russo-Japanese War and in the war against the Central

67

Powers. He was a British protégé—they had transported him to Omsk via Shanghai and Tokyo—but he had also impressed State Department officials during a previous visit to the United States. Perhaps, a number of people hoped, he would be the "strongman" necessary to provide order and direction for the anti-Bolshevik movement.

Kolchak's performance during the first few weeks after the coup gave cause for optimism. He ordered the recruitment of most able-bodied males in areas controlled by his regime which promised to augment greatly the White armies now replacing Czech units at the front. In addition, he made a number of statements indicating that his dictatorship was only a temporary expediency and would in time be replaced by a representative government. There would be no reprisals against other non-Bolshevik factions, he said, and his government would be as liberal as conditions permitted.

In fact the admiral was a reactionary by temperament and training. He tried to crush even the slightest dissent against his heavy-handed methods. Although of course he was not responsible for every incident, he did so little to restrain his subordinates that atrocities against people whose loyalties he presumably was trying to gain became commonplace. His liberal pronouncements, furthermore, seem to have been inspired by one John Sukine rather than being representative of the admiral's views. Sukine, who became Kolchak's minister for foreign affairs, had been sent to Siberia some months earlier by Ambassador Bakhmetev of the Russian embassy in Washington.[5] Whatever his own sentiments, Sukine wished to gain American recognition and open support for Kolchak. He advised the admiral, therefore, to say what he thought the Americans wanted to hear about his intentions.

Analyses of the new regime forwarded to Washington by General Graves and other army officers were accurate from the start. "All information that I am able to obtain," Graves wrote within weeks of the coup, "leads me to the conclusion that the Government, headed by Admiral Kolchak, can not last."[6] They subsequently reported in detail the repressions, atrocities and the government's failure to gain popular support. The forced recruitment—impressment, actually—increased the size of White armies, they pointed out, but meant that large numbers of troops would be unreliable in combat.

This pessimistic view forwarded by military personnel aroused considerable resentment in Washington and conflicted with much of the information received through regular diplomatic channels. The latter tended to ignore or minimize the weaknesses of the Omsk regime and to explain why they would be rectified in the near future. A common theme put forward repeatedly over the months was that Kolchak was a progressive leader surrounded by reactionaries. According to this interpretation, if supported and given enough time, he would replace these men with others more congenial to his real sympathies.

How does one explain these conflicting evaluations? The army personnel, with no previous experience in Russia, showed little bias toward any faction and reported what they observed as best they could. However, since they were stationed in White-controlled territories, they saw only the White atrocities and brutality. Diplomatic sources, on the other hand, often had resided in Russia for extended periods. The people they dealt with, their friends, sometimes even their wives were Russians, and all were dedicated anti-Bolsheviks. Usually far from actual events, the diplomats tended to place the information they received within a preconceived context: the Whites were the forces of law and order, the Reds were bent on the destruction of Russia.

The bias of diplomatic representatives in Russia was shared by their superiors in Washington. Most State Department officials were vehement anti-Bolsheviks, and some advocated open support for anyone who would fight the Reds. They bridled under President Wilson's unwillingness to participate more forcefully in Russian affairs. Even so, they believed General Graves's orders permitted him more latitude than he

THE UNKNOWN WAR WITH RUSSIA

was willing to exercise and came to resent him bitterly. For the remaining period of the intervention there developed in the department (below the level of Secretary Lansing) a concerted effort to have the general replaced by someone more politically oriented.[7]

Although this matter will be discussed more fully in a later chapter, it is worthwhile to note here the role of the military establishment throughout the intervention. In Wilson's cabinet, Secretary of War Newton D. Baker argued the most adamantly against American participation. He was supported by the president's representative on the Allied Supreme War Council, Gen. Tasker H. Bliss, and the United States Army chief of staff, Maj. Gen. Peyton C. March. And, once the intervention was mounted, it was the military which adhered most rigorously to the president's strictures against interference in Russia's domestic struggle. Indeed, General Graves was fortunate to have behind him the men he did. Perfectly aware of the State Department's intrigues, General March on one occasion notified Graves to "keep a stiff upper lip. I am going to stand by you until hell freezes over."[8]

Graves, who knew his conduct was being criticized in Washington, nevertheless adhered to his policy of noninterference. Through the winter of 1918-1919, bad weather hindered the fighting, and there were no significant developments. Small-scale raids and sabotage continued in the Suchan region, and there were incidents involving American and Japanese troops in and around Vladivostok. Often these were no more than individual brawls or inadvertent clashes between patrols, but they did indicate a disharmony among the intervening forces. The coming of spring brought more serious friction.

Even before the Bolshevik Revolution, one of Russia's most serious problems had been the breakdown of its transportation system. The huge stores mounted at Vladivostok because the Russians themselves had been able to move only a fraction of the materials inland. To alleviate this situation, President Wilson had created the American Russian Railway Service

70

Corps. This group of engineers and railroad experts, which was to have placed itself at the disposal of the Provisional Government, had been stranded in Japan when the Bolsheviks seized power. Some members later worked on the Chinese Eastern Railway (an alternate route through Manchuria which connected with the Trans-Siberian east of Chita and north of Vladivostok), but now, in the spring of 1919, President Wilson sought to use the corps to reorganize the Siberian system.

After much haggling among the powers, an agreement was worked out in March 1919 which provided for utilization of the Railway Corps in Siberia. Parts of the agreement, however, bore directly on the military situation. Although American experts would handle technical operations, overall control would be in the hands of Russians. The result was that the Kolchak government would try to use the rails exclusively for its own benefit and would purge the system of anyone suspected of disloyalty. Secondly, the agreement specified the areas to be guarded by the intervening powers, thereby freeing White Russians for combat against the Bolsheviks. Under this arrangement Americans for the first time were sent into the interior of Siberia where they were assigned a section of the line just east of Lake Baikal.

American forces had been bothered for some time by the Japanese-supported Cossack, Kalmikov. Operating around Khabarovsk, Kalmikov had expressed his dislike of the Americans through actions such as throwing dead horses from his trains as they passed through American encampments. But these incidents were mere nuisances. Now, because of the railway agreement, Americans encountered Gregorii Semenov, also a Cossack and also sponsored by the Japanese. Controlling the area around Chita, Semenov acted independently of the Kolchak government and kept his men supplied partly by raiding trains destined for Omsk. Backed by the Japanese and possessing the largest fleet of armored trains in Siberia (the most notorious of these, the *Destroyer* was shielded by steel plate and eighteen inches of reinforced

71

concrete and mounted four cannons as well as many machine guns), Semenov was a bone in Kolchak's throat which the latter could not dislodge.

Two battalions of the Twenty-seventh Infantry, command-ed by Colonel C. H. Morrow, were sent to guard the track in the Baikal area. Morrow, like General Graves, interpreted his orders strictly and permitted no interference with the conduct of his duty. Semenov, who had ranged freely before the Americans arrived, had no intention of curbing his activities. The two clashed almost immediately and on one occasion almost precipitated a small war. Semenov had arrested sev-eral Russian railroad employees, claiming they were Bolshe-viks. When Morrow protested, the Cossack leader sent word that he would do as he pleased and indicated that he meant to seize more Russian personnel. The situation reached its cli-max when Morrow forbade the *Destroyer* to proceed beyond a certain point on the rail line and mounted on both sides of the track 37-millimeter cannon to impress the Russian.

Morrow's courage, if not his judgement, can hardly be questioned. That his small artillery pieces could have serious-ly damaged, let alone stopped, the heavily armored train is doubtful. Nevertheless, when the *Destroyer* appeared, Mor-row informed the Cossacks that if it moved into the American sector he would fire upon it. The showdown grew even more ominous when Japanese troops appeared on the scene. Hav-ing previously informed Morrow that they would not permit him to attack Semenov's train, they now situated themselves so that they would be in the line of American fire if shooting began. Since the Japanese by this time outnumbered the Americans by at least five to one, Morrow knew that his position was hazardous, to say the least.

The colonel refused to budge. Repeating his threat to begin firing on the train should it move forward, he ordered his men to stand ready. The Japanese, at last convinced that Morrow meant what he said, commandeered the train and had it backed down the rail line out of range. This was the first encounter the Cossacks and Japanese had with Morrow, but it would not be the last. "The Japanese regarded Colonel Morrow," a fellow officer later recalled, "as a sort of bomb with the fuse already lighted."*9

The experiences of the A.E.F. in Siberia during the latter part of the intervention will be discussed in a subsequent chapter. But its role as established by General Graves remained unchanged. The very act of guarding the rail lines and coal fields placed American forces in opposition to the Bolsheviks. Their neutral conduct within this framework, however, alienated almost all the other parties involved. Graves refused to lend himself to British and French designs and brooked no interference by the Cossacks or the Japanese. The Kolchak government repeatedly protested against Graves's behavior, criticizing him for his unwillingness to act aggressively against the Reds. These complaints were received sympathetically in the State Department, the middle echelons of which were actively working for his recall.

Although apparently none of these factors affected Graves's conduct, he must at times have wondered precisely what he was expected to accomplish. His original instructions, President Wilson's aide-mémoire, were never altered. Vague even during the war, they were irrelevant to the situation in Siberia after the armistice. "I was in command of the United States troops sent to Siberia," Graves wrote years afterward, "and, I must admit, I do not know what the United States was trying to accomplish by military intervention."10 Presumably President Wilson knew, but it would not have occurred to Graves to question the motives of his commander in chief.

---

*Actually, the situation may have been even more explosive than it appeared at the time. This account of the confrontation, and the quotation about Morrow, appears in a paper read at the Army War College by a Lieutenant Colonel H. H. Slaughter. Slaughter, then a major, was General Graves's representative at Omsk. Slaughter went on to say that a member of the Czech Corps staff later told him that "Czech headquarters was firmly convinced Colonel Morrow would have to fight the Japanese and they had a troop movement schedule all prepared which would have brought 10,000 Czechs to Colonel Morrow's aid in two days." One can only speculate on the chaos such an internecine struggle among the intervening powers would have produced.

Woodrow Wilson and the Russian Civil War

5

The most dramatic consequence of the armistice in November, 1918, was that it ended more than four years of fighting on the western front. It should have affected the Siberian situation as well, many people believed, for the announced purpose of the intervention was to protect the Czechs and Russians from the Central Powers. In fact the cessation of hostilities changed little in Siberia, and the contending forces there in no way altered their behavior. In the months following, President Wilson offered no new reasons for the continued American presence in Russia, even as it elicited more and more criticism from Congress and the press. Some scholars, emphasizing Wilson's reluctance to go along with intervention in the first place, his insistence upon strict American neutrality and his performance at the Paris Peace Conference, have argued that the president was motivated primarily by deference to the wishes of Great Britain and France. But his actions, as opposed to his words, point to a different conclusion: he sought to use intervention to destroy the Bolshevik movement.

Earlier in the year, Wilson had chided the Bolsheviks for their unrealistic economic and social doctrines and for their naiveté in seeking peace with Imperial Germany. The thrust of his remarks, however, had been that the Russians were misguided rather than evil. At that stage, the outcome of the war was by no means certain and it was widely believed that the Communist seizure of power represented a temporary aberration made possible by wartime dislocations. As the war neared its end and as the Bolsheviks consolidated their grip instead of losing it, the president's attitude changed markedly. He began to define bolshevism as a threat not only to Russia, but to Europe and the United States as well. The kind of postwar world he envisioned had no place for extremism on the right *or* the left.

Perhaps the most striking example of Wilson's metamorphosis can be seen in his decision to authorize publication of the so-called Sisson Papers in mid-September 1918. Edgar Sisson was an American journalist who in the fall of 1917 had been sent to Russia by the Committee on Public Information, a wartime propaganda agency. Arriving in Petrograd shortly after the Bolshevik coup, Sisson acquired a set of documents purporting to show that Lenin and Trotsky were paid agents of the German government. Some Americans on the scene dismissed the documents as forgeries, but Sisson, convinced of their authenticity, thought it crucial that they be brought to the attention of higher officials in Washington. Returning to the United States in the spring of 1918, he presented his information to the head of the committee, George Creel. Apparently persuaded that the documents were genuine, Creel authorized Sisson to tell his story to State Department officials and a few days later forwarded Sisson's written report directly to President Wilson. To Sisson's great dismay, he was rebuffed. Although no one directly challenged his allegations, neither did they show any interest in his insistence that his documents be made public. "His attitude," State Department Counselor Frank Polk archly noted in a memorandum of their conversation, "was rather one of a newspaper man who had secured what he thought was the greatest scoop in history and which was not being made use of by his superiors."[1]

The exact circumstances under which the president decided to publish the Sisson Papers four months later remain a mystery. He did so after a conversation with Creel, but without consulting either Colonel House or Secretary of State Lansing. Did he believe the documents to be genuine, as some historians have suggested, thereby justifying intervention as a wartime operation against Germany and the Austro-Hungarian Empire? Or was he trying to discredit the Soviet government by any means available so as to undermine dis-

sent when it became clear that henceforth the goal of intervention (if it were not already) would be to defeat bolshevism?
The president's failure to confer with members of the State
Department—who thought the documents to be spurious and
who presumably were better equipped to judge than George
Creel—makes the latter proposition the more plausible one.
And, though he defended his action to House a few days later
on the ground that he thought the documents authentic,
nothing Wilson said or wrote subsequently indicates that he
actually believed Lenin or Trotsky were German agents.

Whatever his motives, Wilson understood that his decision
to release the Sisson Papers placed the United States in direct
opposition to the Bolsheviks and ended the fiction of neutrality. Lansing and other top officials at the State Department,
militant anti-Bolsheviks all, tried desperately to convince
Wilson to delay publication at least until American personnel
still in Soviet-dominated areas could be evacuated. House,
who told the president he believed the documents were
forgeries, added that their publication amounted to a virtual
declaration of war against the Bolsheviks. "He admitted this,"
House noted in his diary.*[2]

There is ample evidence of Wilson's hardening attitude
toward the Bolsheviks during this period. His recommendation that the Czechs pull back east of the Urals provides a case
in point. In a memorandum to Secretary Lansing on September 26, he stated that "our sympathies constrain us to make
every possible sacrifice to keep the country on the Volga front

---

*Shortly after the documents were published, two noted American scholars were
asked to examine them. They pronounced most of the papers genuine but later
admitted that strong "pressures" had been brought upon them to do so. Today it
seems beyond question that they were forgeries. See George F. Kennan. "The
Sisson Documents," *Journal of Modern History* 28 (June 1956), pp. 130ff. It should
be noted that Lenin and other Bolsheviks did receive subsidies from the German
government before the revolution, for the destruction of the existing government
was as much in the interest of Germany as of the Communists. But this is a far cry
from Sisson's allegation that the Bolshevik leadership followed orders from Berlin.

out of the hands of the merciless Red Guards." His suggestion, he went on, was prompted by purely practical considerations as "it is the unqualified judgment of our military authorities that to attempt that is to attempt the impossible." This is a revealing statement from a man whose professed goals were restricted to getting the Czechs out of Russia and helping the Russians defend themselves against Germany and Austria-Hungary, particularly when one realizes that it was made at a time when the last great Allied offensives which would end the war were already well under way.

Three weeks after his decision to release the Sisson Papers, Wilson explained to a British intelligence officer, Sir William Wiseman, how the specter of bolshevism influenced his thinking about ending the war as quickly as possible. "We should consider too the condition of Germany," he said. "If we humiliate the German people and drive them too far, we shall destroy all form of government there and Bolshevism will take its place."[3] A week before the armistice Wilson again expressed his concern, this time at a cabinet meeting. "The President spoke at length," recalled one member, "of the possibility of revolutions in Europe under the stress of conditions and the influence of Bolshevik propaganda." After some discussion of the matter, Wilson asked Secretary Lansing to confer with American diplomats "to see if European governments would seize Bolshevist funds and expel agitators."[4]

The president's apprehensions about the menace of bolshevism—and his desire to do something about it—can best be seen in the administration's use of the Russian embassy after the intervention began. The embassy, it will be recalled, had served as the Provisional Government's procurement agency and was permitted to continue functioning *after* the Bolshevik Revolution. At first the administration had defended this situation on the ground that the Bolsheviks had seized power illegally and did not represent the Russian people. Later, in reply to growing ciriticism, more pragmatic explanations were offered. The ambassador and his staff, it was explained publicly, actually were working in behalf of the American people.

The Provisional Government had negotiated hundreds of contracts which were in various stages of completion by the time of the November revolution, and abrupt cancellation of these agreements in many cases would inflict severe losses upon American businessmen. The State Department reasonably argued that the contractors involved, having acted in good faith, deserved protection. The embassy's function, henceforth, would be to liquidate its obligations with the least possible dislocation to American firms. Coordinating his moves with the Departments of State and Treasury, Ambassador Bakhmetev was to reduce, transfer, and cancel contracts when possible and resell those goods on which delivery could not be halted. The sums realized by such sales, together with the unspent funds still on deposit, would be applied to the Provisional Government's debt to both the American government and private bankers.

The embassy's conduct belied the official version from the start. It did begin reducing and cancelling contracts for materials which could be of no further use in Russia. Items such as barbed wire, vitally needed elsewhere, were disposed of at handsome prices. But other contracts were not renegotiated at all. An order with the Remington Rifle Company involving 245,000 weapons, for example, was allowed to proceed, even though the first deliveries were not scheduled until July 1918.[5] The embassy's deposits with the First National City Bank of New York bulked larger than any specific transaction. Amounting to at least fifty-six million dollars as of November 1917, these funds represented the unexpended portion of private and government loans. Augmented regularly by the income from sales and other sources, the ostensible purpose of this liquidation account, as it became known, was to help satisfy the Provisional Government's creditors after settlement of the contracts. Instead, it became a source of disbursement under the stewardship of the United States government.

Through these months, the administration worked actively to prevent dissipation of funds through debt payment. For instance, an issue of Russian notes totalling eleven million dollars which had been sold on the American market in 1916 matured on May 1, 1918. While Bakhmetev had sufficient money to redeem the notes, this would have curtailed his ability to fulfill his contractual obligations. The noteholders spurned his offer to meet the interest due in return for a year's extension on the principal, and the National City Bank —whose conduct up to this time had "relieved the government of the United States of grave embarrassment," as one administration official put it—threatened to block expenditures from the liquidation account until the debt was settled. The danger was that, if private investors went to the courts, the administration might have to "take over all Russian assets" in order to satisfy its own claims. Such a move would destroy the embassy's usefulness by removing the funds from its sanctuary. The State Department thereupon intervened and succeeded in having the bankers reverse their decision. To demonstrate that the administration possessed the forbearance it had asked of the financiers, the Treasury Department deferred payment on government loans and permitted Bakhmetev to give IOUs in lieu of cash.[6]

Thus, by the fall of 1918, the administration controlled a functioning procurement and disbursal agency for which it did not have to account either to Congress or to the public. Ostensibly independent, the embassy acted only with the concurrence of the United States government in supplying and arming *both* the Czechs and the White armies. For instance, of the first 100,000 rifles shipped, 25,000 were to be turned over "to the Russian army being formed at Omsk."[7] By late October a second 100,000 were ready to go, a portion of which were sent ahead on credit. "The balance of 35,800 [rifles] will be paid for by the Russian Embassy out of their available funds," the head of the War Trade Board informed Chief of Staff General March. "For political reasons in which the Department of State concurs, it is deemed advisable that these rifles which belong to the Russians should be shipped immediately to Vladivostok."[8] This writer has been unable to determine what, if any, portion of the second shipment was turned over to the Whites, but 175,000 rifles would seem more than ample for the 65,000 Czech troops then in Russia. The embassy also sent machine guns, sidearms and equipment of all kinds, at the same time helping to finance the Railway Corps in reorganizing the Siberian transportation system.

The president employed other tools as well to subvert the Bolsheviks. During the same week that he authorized publication of the Sisson Papers, Wilson named an informal committee of top officials to expedite the procurement and shipping of goods destined for Russia. The committee, which Wilson dubbed his "little war board," consisted of Vance C. McCormick, head of the War Trade Board, Bernard M. Baruch of the War Industries Board, and chairman of the U.S. Shipping Board, Edward N. Hurley.[9] This arrangement was formalized early in November by the creation of the Russian Bureau, Inc., of the War Trade Board under McCormick's direction.

Most scholars have ignored or overlooked the committee and minimized the Russian Bureau's importance. In the latter case, they point out that the bureau was capitalized at only five million dollars and received another five million later— sums scarcely adequate for large operations. But this conclusion misses the point. Although the bureau did purchase and ship some supplies out of its own funds, its primary function (as was the committee's earlier) was to facilitate the Russian embassy's efforts to nourish the Czechs and Whites. Frequently this involved negotiations with private firms but as often as not meant dealing with other agencies of the American government. A common practice, for instance, was to have the War Department declare as "surplus" those items which the embassy wished to purchase. Such transactions made the goods available quickly and at a fraction of their market price. The Russian Bureau then had the responsibility for transporting the materials to port cities and providing the necessary shipping space. The records of the War Trade Board, now located in the National Archives, show that such activities far exceeded the bureau's nominal role.

Wilson's publication of the Sisson Papers, his private remarks about the dangers of bolshevism and the administration's deep involvement with every phase of the Russian embassy's program contrast strikingly with the president's attitude toward the intervention as expressed publicly and to the European Allies. Two factors have obscured Wilson's real aims. First, as pointed out in previous chapters, he was intent upon having it appear that the United States would not involve itself in Russia's political matters, regardless of what actually happened. Second, he had very limited freedom of action, whatever his inclinations. Congressional opposition, muted but powerful for the duration of the war, began breaking out openly during the fall of 1918. Had he requested appropriations for any purpose conceivably involving the conflict in Russia, he would have faced strong resistance, if not defeat, and the very act of justifying his plans would have destroyed the facade of neutrality he strove to maintain. By this time, Wilson placed so high a priority on creating a league of nations that it precluded taking any steps which might jeopardize his already shaky relations with the Senate, through which any treaty providing for league membership would have to pass.

The administration went to great lengths to conceal its true role in the Russian civil war. In response to questions about the activities of the Russian embassy, it replied that the embassy represented a foreign government and was not under American control. Criticisms of American agencies such as the War Trade Board were rebuffed by claims that the United States government furnished only nonmilitary goods to help the Russian people. The latter point was technically true *for those items the War Trade Board purchased and shipped on its own.* No one would surmise, from the statements issued, the administration's direct involvement in arming and provisioning the Czechs and Whites. And, as the records and diaries of State Department officials make clear, this was not something which just "happened"; President Wilson was consulted and informed of these activities on almost a day-to-day basis.

Despite its protestations of innocence, the administration came under increasing fire during the weeks following the armistice. American troops still were in Russia, after all, and more and more people demanded to know what they were doing there and how long they would stay. Early in December, Senator Hiram Johnson of California launched an assault on Wilson's Russian policies. Johnson later told a friend he had "started something" with his Senate speech which he hoped would force the administration into revealing its intentions.[10] What he started was an intermittent debate which lasted until mid-February 1919, when his resolution calling for withdrawal of American forces from Russia was defeated only by Vice-President Thomas Marshall's tie-breaking vote. Wilson's opposition would have been greater had the administration's behind-the-scenes activities been revealed.

Meanwhile, as protests in the Senate heated up, President Wilson departed for Europe to attend the Paris Peace Conference which began in early January. A number of his advisers counseled against his taking part in the actual negotiations, arguing that his enormous personal prestige would be tarnished by the inevitable compromises such negotiations would entail. Wilson refused to limit himself to a ceremonial role, however, believing that he alone commanded the breadth of vision and determination to construct the kind of postwar world he thought would endure. The issues at the conference were bewildering in number and complexity: the treatment of Germany and disposition of her colonies, dismemberment of the Austro-Hungarian Empire, and the creation of a league of nations, among others. But Russia and the menace of bolshevism were never far offstage. "Communist Russia," recalled a member of the American mission, Herbert C. Hoover, "was a specter which wandered into the Peace Conference almost daily."[11]

Unfortunately, for the sake of unity on the Russian question, the nations could not agree on a course of action. Not only were there differences between the delegations, but some were divided internally. President Wilson accepted or rejected advice from his associates as he chose. The British and French delegations, however, represented coalition governments and rarely spoke with one voice. The French Premier Georges Clemenceau, for instance, inclined toward creating a cordon of friendly buffer states between Soviet Russia and the West. At the same time Marshal Ferdinand Foch, a French war hero of considerable influence, persistently argued for an anti-Bolshevik military crusade in which he was willing to enlist even German forces. The British mission was similarly divided. The prime minister, David Lloyd George, vacillated between a moderate approach toward the Bolsheviks which he personally favored and a more militant stance when he felt pressured by conservative members of the War Cabinet. War Minister Winston Churchill had the virtue of consistency: like Foch, he wished to destroy bolshevism through force of arms. Churchill added to the confusion by presenting his own proposals during the prime minister's absences from the conference and by his tireless lobbying for his projects.

Russia and communism would have posed a dilemma even if there had been more cohesiveness among and within the delegations. Theoretically the Big Four could have treated Russia in a variety of ways ranging from full recognition of the

Soviet regime to an all-out military offensive against it.* Practical considerations precluded either approach. With widespread social upheavals in Eastern and Central Europe raising the threat of Bolshevik successes there, and given the states of opinion toward communism within the Allied nations, few members of the conference were willing to advocate recognition even if they favored it, which most did not. As for a large-scale intervention, the question invariably bogged down over the matter of who would provide the enormous amounts of troops and materials necessary. The Allied nations were desperately weary of war, and the prospect of mounting another military effort brought the disquieting possibility of troop mutinies, riots and falling governments. Even ardent interventionists like Foch and Churchill mumbled vaguely about volunteers and mercenaries when asked how in fact their schemes could be implemented.

Unwilling either to recognize the Soviet regime as the government of Russia or to mount an invasion against it, moderates cast about for a workable alternative. Some wished to effect a truce among the warring factions in order to stop the bloodshed and lay the foundation for a negotiated settlement. Presumably they hoped to establish either a network of coexisting regional structures or a national coalition government in which the Bolsheviks were one of several parties. Implicit in this approach was the notion that, if treated decently, the Bolsheviks would become more "responsible" and abandon their radical doctrines. Other members of the peace conference wanted to render more effective what was already being done: arming, supplying and advising anti-Communist forces in hopes that they could defeat the Bolsheviks outright.

*The Big Four—the United States, Great Britain, France and Italy (with the last decidedly a junior partner)—made the major decisions about Russia, although the subject at times was discussed in the Council of Ten. Japan was largely excluded from such deliberations even though it had the largest contingent in Russia.

Accomplishing this, they predicted, would undercut the menace of radicalism in all of Europe.

Concensus was difficult to reach for a number of reasons. Treating with the Bolsheviks, even as one of several de facto regimes, was sure to stir up the right at home, just as continuing the intervention would further arouse the left. Could the Bolsheviks be tamed or would they use a truce to improve their position and to sow discord in other areas? On the other hand, if support for the Whites were stepped up, would they be able to set aside their many differences to achieve a united front against the Reds? And finally, what kind of Russia did the Allies wish to emerge? President Wilson wanted to maintain the territorial integrity of the prewar Russian Empire, with the exception of Poland, but for various reasons some of his subordinates and most of the European delegates sought to dismember it.

Between January and March, the conference made several tentative gestures toward accommodation with the Bolsheviks, though with much foot-dragging, particularly on the part of the French. First was the Prinkipo Islands Conference, a proposed meeting between representatives of the Allied and Associated Powers and delegations from all the Russian factions.* Wilson himself drafted the invitation, which stated that the goal of the conference was to ascertain "the wishes of all sections of the Russian people, and bringing about, if possible, some understanding and agreement by which Russia may work out her own purposes."[12] Whether reconciliation among groups ranging from monarchists to Bolsheviks could have been achieved can only be guessed, for the conference was never held. The White regimes refused to participate and the Soviet reply contained passages which even

---

*The site, a group of islands near Constantinople, was chosen to provide an isolated, neutral ground for the meeting. There had been some talk of inviting the delegations to Paris, but Clemenceau vetoed the idea because the French right would have been outraged by the appearance of a Bolshevik delegation.

the most earnest advocate of conciliation had to admit were insulting. Yet, as John M. Thompson has pointed out, the Allies themselves bore part of the blame.[13] They neither pressed the Whites, who could not survive without them, nor did they follow up the portions of the Bolshevik reply which indicated that the latter were genuinely ready to negotiate.

The so-called Bullitt mission represented another abortive attempt to treat with the Bolsheviks. William C. Bullitt, a young member of the American commission, was authorized by Colonel House (with President Wilson's concurrence) to confer with Bolshevik leaders in Russia about the conditions necessary to obtain an end to the fighting. The origins of the trip and the discussions held are too complex to be detailed here, but it ended in failure. Bullitt, believing he had been empowered to conduct formal negotiations with the Soviets, had obtained a series of agreements which he thought would be favorably received by the Allies.[14] The president, on the other hand, apparently viewed the mission as an exploratory one. Because of a number of events which occurred between the decision to send Bullitt and receipt of the terms he had negotiated, Wilson and the British shied away from pursuing the matter.

The Prinkipo proposal, the Bullitt mission and several relief programs suggested at the peace conference were all abandoned without positive results. French opposition, fear of domestic repercussions and their personal distaste for bolshevism prevented Wilson and Lloyd George from launching any sustained efforts which might have had some chance of success. As Lansing put it in a confidential cable to State Department Counselor Polk:

> *The action taken in regard to the Russian factions was the direct consequence of a recognition of the impossibility of military intervention. . . . In these circumstances the best and humane thing to do seemed to be to make an appeal to the warring ele-*

> *ments to cease violence while the Peace Conference is*
> *in session. . . . It very probably will not accomplish*
> *anything but we could not do less than make an*
> *attempt to stay the slaughter and horror which the*
> *Russians are enduring. The only alternative since*
> *force was out of the question was to remain silent and*
> *let things take their course. That would have satisfied*
> *no one.* 15

Lansing was referring to the Prinkipo proposal, of course, but his diagnosis fit the other gestures as well. There is no reason to believe that Wilson or Lloyd George acted hypocritically, but if they "could not do less," they most certainly were unwilling to do more.

While Foch and Churchill continued to present their sometimes far-fetched schemes for a large-scale invasion of Russia and while Lloyd George and Wilson backed and filled over conciliation, the existing intervention went on as before. No one was very enthusiastic about it because it had produced a great deal of wrangling among the Allies without tangible results. Wilson spoke of it in much the same way he had before the original expedition: no one could send enough forces to defeat the Bolsheviks militarily, and an unsuccessful intervention was worse than none at all. Not only did the Soviets capitalize on the reaction against foreign interference but they pointed to it as proof that the Allies meant to restore the monarchy. The president said perhaps the best thing to do was for everyone to get out, letting the Russians "fight it out themselves," but added that he would not withdraw American troops peremptorily.16 Wilson maintained his attitude of reluctant acquiescence for some time.

But Wilson's actions, even during the early months of the peace conference, belied the indifference he exhibited at the negotiating table. In January, he had cabled Polk to approach Congress for appropriations, a move from which he had studiously refrained in the past. The funds apportioned by the

Russian embassy and the president himself for repairing and improving the Trans-Siberian railway had run out. Wilson thought a persuasive appeal might be made for the railroad which would not bear the onus of interference. He was disappointed. Polk replied that the mood of Congress was such that "no funds for any purpose in Russia" would be forthcoming. When the president persisted, asking Polk to meet confidentially with selected congressmen to plead the cause, the acting secretary restated his opinion more emphatically. Having polled the cabinet and other officials, he said, it was certain not only that appropriations were impossible but that a fight over them would endanger other bills. With the obstacles confronting him reaffirmed, Wilson withdrew his request.[17]

That the president sought funds to continue operations, even while expressing his wish to withdraw, does not mean that he favored the status quo. Rather, it indicates that he wanted to alter the situation instead of merely abandoning it. The extremely unpopular Kolchak regime had alienated the Russian people wherever its forces were located. Observers reported that while the admiral himself seemed acceptable enough, the clique around him was responsible for widespread oppression. Considering himself more sympathetic than his fellow delegates to the "causes which produced Bolshevism," the president thought it self-defeating to help perpetuate the forces of reaction. But he knew also that the militant anti-communism of men like Clemenceau, Foch and Churchill compelled them to support the admiral regardless of the type of government he represented. Wilson believed that if the intervention were to work at all, it would have to be in behalf of a liberal regime which could attract the loyalties of the Russian masses.

When during March and April Kolchak's armies achieved a series of victories over the Reds, Wilson pressed his views. Allied delegates, particularly the militants, clamored for more support for Kolchak and talked about recognizing his regime as the legitimate government of Russia. Wilson still held back.[18] By appearing disenchanted, yet making it obvious that he would be more interested in a liberalized Omsk regime, the president contrived to euchre the Allies into insisting that reorganization precede recognition. He believed this afforded the sole basis for victory.

Wilson's strategy worked. On May 26, 1919, the Allied and Associated Powers notified Kolchak of their willingness to assist him with "munitions, supplies and food," provided he agreed to a number of reforms enumerated in the dispatch. The message made no formal promise of recognition but implied that it would follow implementation of the terms since the stated purpose of the aid was to help him establish a government representing "all Russia."[19] When David Lloyd George remarked that the United States would have to furnish the greater part of the assistance, Wilson replied that the matter was for Congress to decide. He said he thought he could induce Congress to "take a share," if given the opportunity to explain the situation properly—presumably after Kolchak had initiated the reforms and after the Versailles Treaty had passed the Senate.[20]

Once again the dichotomy between Wilson's conduct and his statements before the conference indicates that his commitment to intervention ran deeper than he was willing to acknowledge openly. Just as the note to Kolchak was being drafted, for instance, the Russian embassy faced another crisis. This time payments due threatened the embassy's entire program, raising the possibility that twenty-five million dollars' worth of supplies earmarked for Kolchak might be attached by creditors. The State Department cabled the Commission to Negotiate Peace for instructions, asking whether the department should "lend its good offices to assist the Russian Ambassador in safeguarding Russian assets." After discussing the matter with the president, Lansing replied that the probability of recognizing the Omsk government had "so much increased that . . . it appears more important than ever to continue this policy and avoid the collapse of Russian finance in America at the present"—an interesting response from a man who advocated withdrawal.[21]

The interpretation presented here is not meant to suggest that Wilson travelled to Paris possessing some sort of master plan for Russia. It does suggest, however, that his repugnance for bolshevism precluded any real accommodation with the Soviet government. Between January and March, when the civil war was stalemated, he agreed to some overtures to the Reds but drew back before anything could come of them. Even during this period he continued to support the Russian embassy's program and for the first time considered going to Congress for funds. Then, when it appeared at last that Kolchak was beginning to overcome the Bolsheviks, Wilson joined the Allies in openly pledging support for the Omsk government provided it instituted reforms. As before, the president's attitude towards intervention was shaped less by abstract moral standards than by its prospects for success.

Caught in the Middle

6

While the peacemakers at Versailles groped for a solution to the Russian problem, the foreign contingents in Siberia pursued their separate and conflicting objectives. The British and French carried on their struggle for influence over the Kolchak government, each in their own way seeking to strengthen it against the Bolsheviks. The Japanese, on the other hand, continued their obstructionist tactics, most obviously by subsidizing divisive figures like Semenov and Kalmikov. And although they had evacuated some units during the winter, the Japanese still retained the second largest non-Russian army in Siberia, outnumbered only by the Czechs. Additionally, General Graves's policy of strict neutrality added to the mix yet another ingredient, one which almost everyone else found unpalatable. The Kolchak movement probably would have failed anyway because of its own ineptitude, but in view of such conditions the wonder is that it survived as long as it did.

During the spring of 1919, implementation of the railway agreement providing for the operation and security of the Trans-Siberian railway complicated Graves's position immeasurably. Under the terms of this plan, two battalions of the Twenty-seventh Infantry were transferred to the interior just east of Lake Baikal. Not only did this bring Americans into direct contact with Semenov for the first time, it also further strained relations between Graves and the Omsk regime.

Kolchak had resented American neutrality from the beginning, and his representatives in eastern Siberia had plagued Graves with steady criticism of his conduct. The westward movement of American units threatened to cause a complete rupture. Troops from other nations were properly anti-Bolshevik, Kolchak's spokesmen protested, while the Americans

acted as though there were no difference between the bar-
baric Reds and the Omsk regime which represented the real
Russia. They maintained that the situation was bad enough
already and that stationing such divisive forces so near Omsk
was completely unacceptable, as it would undermine the
regime's claims to legitimacy. Undoubtedly emboldened by
the success of his spring offensive, Kolchak claimed he could
achieve more without the American presence and bluntly
stated that United States troops should be evacuated if they
refused to cooperate.

The admiral's complaints, which were forwarded to the
State Department by Ambassador Bakhmetev in Washington
and to the American delegation at Versailles by Omsk representatives in Paris, precipitated a concerted effort to have
Graves relieved of his command. The British and French also
lodged protests against the general's conduct; on one occasion
David Lloyd George broached the matter directly with President Wilson. Those American officials who wished to extend
formal recognition to Kolchak joined the campaign. In both
Washington and Paris they did what they could to engineer
Graves's recall. As acting secretary Frank Polk put it in a
letter to Lansing, "Graves is a useless old woman."[1]

Graves himself admitted that there was some justification
for the Omsk regime's resentment. Of all the nations participating in the intervention, he believed, the United States was
the one most admired by the Russian people. Its failure to
cooperate militarily with Kolchak implied disapproval of his
policies, thereby impairing his ability to attract more popular
support. The situation was critical, Graves concluded, for "we
will almost surely have armed conflict with Russian troops as
they are determined we cannot remain in Siberia and continue the policy of noninterference." In forwarding Graves's
report to Paris, Secretary of War Baker agreed that the present situation could not continue. "Either General Graves
should be directed to cooperate with the Kolchak govern-

ment," he warned the president, "or he ought to be with-drawn."[2]

Kolchak's resentment of Graves can also be understood in view of the conduct of other American officials in Siberia. American Consul General Ernest L. Harris at Irkutsk and Consul John K. Caldwell at Vladivostok both advocated co-operation with Kolchak, as did other diplomatic personnel. A high-ranking member of the War Trade Board, August Heid, was stationed in Vladivostok where he worked closely with Omsk authorities in shipping materials to the West. Finally, the American Red Cross representative in Siberia, Dr. Rudolf Teusler, used Red Cross auspices to supply Kolchak's forces with three hundred thousand sets of underwear, medical supplies of all kinds, and enough equipment to maintain several field hospitals.[3] To Graves's embarrassment, Teusler spoke often and openly about the necessity of supporting Kolchak as an alternative to communism. The widely known fact that Teusler was Mrs. Wilson's cousin, Graves noted, caused people to treat his views more seriously "than they would have if he had not been so related."[4] Given this situa-tion, Kolchak and Graves's other critics understandably may have thought that the general alone was out of step with the true policy of the American government.

Fortunately for Graves, Secretary Baker and General Bliss stoutly defended him to the president. His conduct had been above reproach, they argued, and he had carried out his instructions to the letter.[5] Wilson agreed and in the face of mounting criticism refused to censure or relieve the belea-gured general. The ultimate responsibility for Graves's pre-dicament, of course, rested squarely with the president. He still did not see a satisfactory solution. Open American in-volvement in the Russian civil war, which he wished to avoid anyway, would arouse a storm of protest at home. Evacuation from Siberia, on the other hand, would undermine the anti-Bolsheviks and facilitate Japanese domination of eastern Siberia. In Wilson's mind this left no choice except to have Graves see it through as best he could. Nevertheless, evidence indicates that the president hoped the joint communiqué of May 26, promising Kolchak aid and assistance, would ameliorate Graves's situation. Perhaps the Omsk officials would become more conciliatory rather than jeopardize the prospects of full support by the Allied and Associated Powers.

Although complaints about Graves's neutral conduct persisted until the end of intervention, Kolchak backed away from his "fight the Reds or get out" ultimatum. Whether he was influenced by the Versailles communiqué or by his own sagging military fortunes (the spring offensive bogged down in a matter of weeks) is uncertain. Perhaps he had been bluffing all the while. Friction between the American military and the Omsk government continued, but the open confrontation Graves feared did not occur.

In addition to the disputes with Kolchak, Semenov and Kalmikov, American forces during late spring of 1919 came under increasing harassment by partisan forces along the rail lines. These clashes were mostly on a very small scale: a sentry killed, a patrol ambushed, shots fired at a passing train. The most troublesome area, as it had been from the start, was the route east from Vladivostok to the Suchan coal mines. American units stationed along the way moved back and forth constantly, trying to prevent the destruction of tracks and bridges. Occasionally they made sweeps through nearby villages, searching for arms and explosives, but these forays usually were unproductive. Most disconcerting to the troops was their realization that the men who tried to kill them at night often were the same individuals who greeted them amiably during the day. In several instances, the soldiers discovered that the unreliable homemade grenades tossed at them were constructed from American tobacco tins. The Americans who had given them as gestures of goodwill were puzzled and angered by the manner in which they were returned.

100

The most costly incident took place at the town of Romanovka, located about halfway between Vladivostok and the
railroad's mountain terminus at Kanghaus.[6] A force of about
seventy-five men from the Thirty-first Regiment was stationed there to patrol a sector of the line. Early on the
morning of June 25, a fairly large group of partisans mounted
a surprise attack on the encampment and took a fearful toll.
This engagement became known to the men of the A.E.F. in
Siberia as the Romanovka Massacre.

The soldiers' tents were clustered between the edge of
town and the railway running past it. Across the tracks rose a
small bluff overlooking the entire area. Sentries posted atop
the bluff were considered sufficient protection against surprise assaults—which, in any event, were not anticipated as
previous encounters had involved only small numbers of men.
Assuming there was little danger to so large an encampment,
sentries standing the last watch habitually left their posts as
soon as it grew light. Since daybreak came early that time of
year, the camp was left unguarded for more than an hour
between the sentries' retirement and reveille. This careless-
ness had not gone unnoticed.

Shortly after dawn on June 25, a large band of partisans
quietly took up positions along the bluff across from the camp.
After allowing sufficient time for the guards to get undressed
and into bed, they opened fire on the unsuspecting Americans. Volley after volley poured into the tents; some men
were hit as they lay sleeping, others as they reached for boots
and weapons. For a time there was chaos, and most of the
casualties were sustained during the first few minutes of the
attack. Fortunately for the Americans, the partisans had no
automatic weapons and many of their rifles were single shot.
Since there was little cover in the camp itself, survivors of the
first volleys crowded into several log cabins which lay immediately to their rear. From there they returned the fire, but
the danger was far from over. Many of the men had been
unable to bring their rifles, and ammunition was limited to

that which had been grabbed on the run. Without reinforcements, the Romanovka detachment faced being surrounded and annihilated.

Second Lieutenant Lawrence D. Butler, who had taken charge of the defense despite being wounded in the lower jaw, asked for volunteers to bring help. Cpl. Louis Heinzman was chosen to try to break out of the trap. Although shot in the ankle, Heinzman escaped through the partisan field of fire and made his way along the tracks toward Kanghaus. Luckily for his waiting comrades, the corporal flagged down a train which otherwise would have blundered into the ambush. The engineer backed down the line to the nearest camp, where reinforcements were hastily assembled on board. The Americans at Romanovka were rescued about four hours after the initial attack. Nineteen men had been killed, five more lay dying, and another twenty-five were wounded—some hideously, from the heavy-caliber, low-velocity weapons used against them. Among the partisan dead were recognized the village shoe repairman and a man who had sold the American troops fresh milk.

The attackers have been referred to in this account as partisans, for their political loyalties are unclear. They may have belonged to any one of the several factions who opposed the Kolchak regime and the presence of foreign troops on Russian soil. Americans in the field rarely made distinctions, however, and blamed the "Reds" for Romanovka. Indeed, it is plain from the many existing accounts of service in Siberia that American soldiers, whatever their officers might have told them, were convinced they were there to combat bolshevism. This feeling can most easily be demonstrated by the songs which became popular around the camps. One, sung to the tune of "The Battle Hymn of the Republic," ran as follows:

We came out from Vladivostok to catch the Bolshevik
We chased them o'er the mountains and we chased them
    through the creek

We chased them every Sunday and we chased them
   through the week
But we couldn't catch a gosh darn one.

Another, its tune unidentified, went:

The bullets may whistle, the cannons may roar
I don't want to go to the trenches no more
Take me over the sea
Where the Bolsheviks can't get at me
Oh my, I don't want to die
I want to go home.

   The incident at Romanovka could have been disastrous for President Wilson's policy toward Russia. Had the entire detachment been wiped out and news of it reached the press, domestic reaction would have been difficult to contain. The administration at that very time was trying to defend the American presence in Siberia before a congressional investigative committee. A larger tragedy at Romanovka would have greatly stimulated criticism of Wilson's failure to remove United States troops from Russia after the armistice. It would have damaged the administration's stance on the pending league of nations issue as well, for some opponents already were pointing to the intervention as a preview of things to come should the United States join that organization.

   Although on a smaller scale than at Romanovka, incidents between American forces and armed Russian bands took place throughout the summer. The American position was awkward, to say the least. United States troops did not engage in the ruthless tactics employed by Kolchak and the Japanese, yet Graves's "neutrality" could not negate the fact that the men under his command were guarding vital transportation facilities, the sole beneficiary of which was the Omsk government. To the anti-Kolchak groups, whoever aided the enemy *was* the enemy.

American clashes with the partisans failed to placate the admiral, of course, who wanted the United States to fight openly on his side. Kolchak's government refrained from issuing any more ultimata after the Versailles decision to increase Allied material support, but Omsk representatives in eastern Siberia continued to harass and ridicule American forces at every opportunity. Pro-Kolchak newspapers in Vladivostok, for instance, printed stories about the alleged Bolshevik leanings of American soldiers. Some of these reports were blatantly anti-Semitic, charging that the A.E.F. in Siberia was composed largely of "Jews of the worst sort." On one occasion Kolchak's highest-ranking agent informed Graves that such propaganda would be stopped upon receipt of money.[7] The general declined, and his already low opinion of the Kolchak regime sank further.

Early in July, Graves received word from Washington that the American ambassador to Japan, Roland S. Morris, would shortly arrive in Vladivostok en route to Omsk. Furthermore, Graves himself was instructed to accompany the ambassador on his trip. Graves at first protested, arguing that his presence in Omsk would be construed as a gesture of support for Kolchak, thus undermining the position of neutrality the general had worked so hard to maintain. His objection was overruled. The matter thus settled, Graves decided to use the opportunity to learn as much as possible about the political and military situation in western Siberia.

On July 11, Morris, Graves, their staffs and interpreters began the long journey. After travelling north for about sixty miles, their train turned west along the Chinese Eastern Railway and carried them across northern Manchuria, a distance of more than 900 miles. Beyond the border of Manchuria a spur line joined with the Trans-Siberian at the city of Karymskaya, just east of Chita. From Chita the train moved west, dipped south around the shore of Lake Baikal and then went on to Omsk. It was a long, exhausting trip, covering approximately 3,700 miles. For Graves, however, it was an enlightening experience. Both he and Ambassador Morris had instructed their interpreters to talk with as many people as they could during the stops in central and western Siberia. Neither found, Graves recalled Morris as saying, "a single individual who spoke a good word for the Kolchak regime."[8]

Graves got along well with the ambassador, regarding him as the least biased of the diplomatic officials with whom he had dealt. Yet Graves's memoirs clearly reveal that the ambassador did not inform him of the precise nature of his mission. That Morris was there to assess the strength and viability of the Omsk government was obvious, but what Graves did not know was that the ambassador was also to impress upon Kolchak the need for reform as a condition of open support and possibly formal recognition.* Finally, Morris was to estimate Kolchak's military needs for the coming year. After a series of meetings with members of the Omsk government and the heads of the French and British military missions, Generals Janin and Knox, Morris cabled Washington his recommendations. These included: 400,000 additional rifles, uniforms for 600,000 men, 3,000 machine guns and 500,000,000 rounds of ammunition. Some of these materials would be paid for by the Russian embassy in Washington, the rest would be "ceded to the Russian Government [Omsk] on favorable conditions of credit."[9]

Graves may have been excluded from these sessions because of his frequently expressed criticisms of the Kolchak regime. In any case, he decided to learn for himself what the military situation really was by visiting the front. This was no easy task. Kolchak's generals obstructed him from the start, putting forth a variety of reasons for refusing him permission to inspect one place or another. Often the people he wanted to see were taking protracted "naps" which could not be

*Nor did Graves know that Morris was ordered by the president to determine "whether it would relieve unnecessary friction at Vladivostok if someone else should take the place of General Graves."[10]

interrupted. Persevering, Graves finally received word that he could go to Ishim, a town on the northernmost sector of the front. Leaving Morris to his negotiations, the general boarded their train and began the journey of about 160 miles.

The trip was most informative. Partway there the mission was halted at a small town, and a group of Kolchak's officers told the American in charge of the guard that the train would be taken over and used for military purposes. Using General Graves's interpreter, the soldier replied to the effect that if anyone tried to come aboard "there would be more dead Russian officers in that town than they had ever seen." The train was permitted to proceed without further interruption. Graves's reception at Ishim was not much warmer. The local commander treated him discourteously and told him there were neither escorts nor motor vehicles available to take him to the front lines. But Graves was a hard man to stop. There was an American automobile on the train and, together with two officers and his interpreters, the general set out on his own.[11]

To simplify an involved story, Graves never found any front lines. He met groups of White soldiers along the roads and motley garrisons in the towns. All seemed lethargic and dispirited, without any real discipline. In Omsk, Graves had been told that Kolchak's forces planned to launch a massive offensive all along the lines within two weeks. The conditions he saw convinced him this was impossible. When at last the general returned to his train and then to Omsk, he confronted the officer who had suggested that he visit Ishim in the first place. The Russian informed Graves, rather lamely one imagines, that he had just missed Kolchak's northern army about ten miles beyond the route Graves had taken. The general did not believe him, and with good reason, for there was no major White offensive in two weeks, or ever. "The fact that Kolchak forces had melted away," Graves cabled Washington after his return to Vladivostok, "was confirmed by many people later seen at Omsk." One informant, Graves continued, "stated that there had been hardly any fighting for nearly six weeks, that the Army had disintegrated, and the men had become worse in their treatment of the inhabitants than the Bolsheviks had ever been."[12]

The train carrying Ambassador Morris and General Graves arrived in Vladivostok on September 6. Trouble awaited. Upon reaching his office Graves learned that an American captain and a corporal had been arrested by some of Kalmikov's troops at Iman, about 250 miles north of Vladivostok.* The next morning Graves sent his chief of staff, Colonel Robinson, to see Kolchak's military commander in the Far East, General Rozanov. Robinson demanded that Rozanov intervene to have the men released. Meanwhile, however, an American officer nearer the scene took matters into his own hands. Maj. Charles A. Shamotulski of the Twenty-seventh Infantry took a detachment of 150 men to Iman to force release of the prisoners. There, what loomed as an ugly confrontation was avoided when he learned that the two men had earlier been taken to Khabarovsk and were no longer in the area. The captain, released very quickly, was unharmed. But when the enlisted man was returned a few days later, he was found to have been badly beaten by the Cossacks.

The incident almost precipitated a major crisis. Graves let it be known that if anything similar happened again, he would hold Kalmikov personally responsible. The general heard from several sources, moreover, that the arrest of the two Americans was but the opening act of a Cossack attempt to "drive the Americans out of Siberia." To make matters worse, according to these sources, Semenov had informed Kalmikov of his willingness to cooperate in this effort. It seemed to Graves that any day might bring open warfare between the widely scattered American forces and the two Cossack groups which were nominally under Admiral Kolchak's control. Aside

---

*Their crime was that they were found without passports, something no soldier in uniform possessed.

from endangering the lives of the men under his command, such a conflict would have brought chaos to Siberia.

At precisely this time, the first shipment of rifles sent directly by the American government (rather than through the Russian embassy) under the Versailles agreement arrived in Vladivostok. However, when Kolchak's ordnance officer appeared to make partial payment and take possession of these weapons, Graves refused to turn them over. On September 16, he cabled his reasons to the War Department:

> Reference to your 357, the one million gold was offered to me this morning and delivery of rifles requested. On account of anti-American actions of Kolchak agents here, Semenov, Kalmikov and Roza-nov, I have refused to take the gold and have refused to give up the rifles. Request approval of this action. Mr. Morris here and approved. I have told [Major] Slaughter to tell Omsk Government we will not give them any Military supplies, as long as Kolchak agents in the East, are threatening to use Military force against the United States. [13]

Graves's action stirred up a furor in the State Department. "It ought to cost the General his head," one high official wrote to another, "and I am doing my best to make it so."[14] Graves's refusal to turn over the weapons, he concluded, "was most insulting, and the Omsk government has naturally come to the conclusion that we have deserted them." Confided another official to his diary, "Siberia has more or less blown up. . . . Gen'l Graves has sent a note to the Omsk foreign office, totally without his jurisdiction and in flagrant violation of the policy laid down by the President. . . . So we have recommended Graves' recall."[15] There is reason to believe that someone in the department leaked the story to the press in a way that reflected badly on Graves: that his act had been motivated solely by the wish to retaliate against the anti-American articles appearing in Vladivostok newspapers, rather than by his concern about the safety of American troops. To those who had wished to get rid of Graves all along, this incident seemed to afford the perfect opportunity.

Several factors worked in Graves's favor. First, as some members of the State Department quickly realized, the general's removal so soon after the beating of an American soldier could easily backfire.[16] If the story became public, and most likely it would, Graves would appear to have been sacrificed because he had tried to protect the men under his command. Second, Secretary of War Baker again threw his influence behind the general, personally defending him to the president.

The result was a standoff. Graves kept his command but was told in what amounted to a reprimand that henceforth he should communicate with the Omsk government only through regular diplomatic channels. As for the rifles, Secretary Baker cabled Graves that President Wilson "feels that his agreement to support Kolchak, made in Paris, ought to be carried out if possible." Delivery, therefore, was "highly desirable," provided Graves could make sure the weapons would reach Omsk and not fall into the hands of Kalmikov or Semenov. If the rifles were not handed over, Baker concluded somewhat ominously, "cable at once reasons why."[17]

Still, the affair was not over. Interpreting his orders literally, as was his wont, Graves decided that the only way to make certain that all the rifles reached Omsk was to send them in trains guarded exclusively by Americans. He would deliver the weapons at Irkutsk, Graves told Kolchak's ordnance man, a city well to the west of the areas dominated by Kalmikov and Semenov. This change infuriated Kolchak's military representatives, as Graves must have foreseen, because of the implication that the Omsk government was unable to protect its own supplies from the Cossack chieftains.

The first trainload of rifles reached Irkutsk without incident. The second was not so fortunate. Commanded by Lieutenant P. A. Ryan with a detachment of fifty men, the train was halted at Chita by Semenov's troops. They demanded

15,000 rifles and, when the lieutenant refused, brought up two armored cars and a battalion of Cossacks. Ryan wired his plight to Graves, who ordered him not to move and to fire only in self-defense. For some forty hours the train stood surrounded while the nervous Americans wondered whether they would get out alive. Colonel Morrow of the Twenty-seventh Infantry, camped closer to Chita than Graves, made it clear to all that he would welcome orders to move on the city.* At last convinced the Americans would not be bluffed, Semenov allowed the train to resume its journey. In the end, however, Graves's precautions were in vain, for he found out later that Kolchak had sent some of the rifles back to Semenov after their delivery in Irkutsk.

Although incidents between the Americans and Cossacks continued, the large-scale clash Graves had feared did not materialize. Probably the general exaggerated the danger, mistaking rhetoric for statements of intent, but he could not overlook even the slightest possibility of Cossack attacks upon his men. Then too, the fortunes of war west of Omsk may have had a restraining influence on Kalmikov and Semenov. White armies, having stood briefly during August and September (though the great offensive predicted by Omsk officials never came off), resumed their retreat in October. By the middle of that month the Czechs, who had been guarding a substantial portion of the Trans-Siberian railway between Omsk and Lake Baikal, announced that they were preparing to move east to Vladivostok. This rapidly deteriorating situation probably gave Semenov and Kalmikov second thoughts about pushing the Americans too far. Indeed, three weeks after the Chita incident, Graves was informed that "the Cossacks desired to let the past die in so far as Americans were

---

*Semenov had encountered Morrow a few months earlier, it will be remembered, when the colonel had ordered a Cossack armored train out of the American sector. According to one version of the Chita incident, Semenov sent Morrow a telegram soon after Ryan's train was released. "Dear Colonel: We understand each other," it ran, "I see, don't worry. I shake your hand."[18]

concerned and [to] establish friendly relations." When an officer representing Semenov visited Graves to explain this conversion, the general brusquely replied that the United States claimed the right "to have no dealings with Russians who committed acts opposed to all moral laws."[19]

The White position continued to erode. By mid-November, almost a year after he had seized power, Kolchak abandoned Omsk to advancing Red armies. Almost immediately an insurrection against his authority broke out in Vladivostok. It was a curious affair, headed by one of the more colorful characters to emerge during this period, Gen. Radula Gaida. A Czech in his late 20s, Gaida had been a junior officer in the legion only a year and a half earlier. Courageous, strongwilled and rash, Gaida had risen rapidly in the legion during its campaigns against the Bolsheviks. When the Czechs took up guard duty in the rear, however, Gaida resigned and became one of Kolchak's generals. The young Czech broke with Kolchak during the summer retreat of 1919, openly criticizing the corruption and inefficiency of the Omsk government. Gaida arrived in Vladivostok early in August, and rumors soon began circulating that he was conspiring with anti-Kolchak groups in the city. Why General Brazanov refused to take action, Graves was unable to determine. Possibly, he was reluctant to antagonize the Czechs, even though Gaida was no longer a member of the legion.*

The uprising began on November 16 and lasted two days. On the seventeenth, the Allied commanders, including Graves, met to discuss what, if any, action they should take. Their decision was to stay neutral and to use their troops only to prevent looting and arson. Graves witnessed some of the fighting from his bedroom window, for Kolchak troops had set up a machine gun at a nearby intersection. Gaida's support-

---

*Rozanov's treatment of the rebels who survived points to this conclusion. The few Czechs who were involved, including Gaida himself, were turned over to Czech headquarters in Vladivostok. Most of the Russians captured were immediately shot.

ers, firing from concealment, quickly shot down the gunners. Graves was amazed that the Russians neither removed the gun nor attempted to protect it. Instead, one after another, replacements manned the weapon until they too were killed. All this was done, Graves recalled, "without any excitement."[20] The short-lived revolt ended in the early hours of November 18. Surrounded and cut off at the railway station where they had taken refuge, Gaida and his followers put down their arms.

Although Kolchak's troops had won, the Gaida insurrection was a portent. The Omsk government had ruled the areas it occupied by force. Because of its incompetence and excesses, Kolchak's regime had failed to gain the loyalties of the war-weary masses or even of its own armed forces. Propped up by foreign troops, money and supplies, it survived because its enemy was weak. The Bolsheviks, struggling to forge both a new society and a revolutionary army, were forced to disperse their strength on several fronts. Their effectiveness, such as it was, was made possible only by the deficiencies of their opponents. Kolchak's regime began coming apart not merely because of its military reverses but because it had failed to attract support from the Russian people. The admiral's downfall, which General Graves had predicted from the start, was fast approaching.

End
of An
Illusion

7

President Wilson returned from Paris in the spring of 1919 determined above all to secure acceptance of the Versailles Treaty containing the League of Nations Covenant. Success would have enabled him to set in motion his plans for Russia. When opponents of the league, led by Henry Cabot Lodge, decided upon the strategy of delaying senatorial consideration of the treaty, however, they inadvertently exercised a veto over Russian policy throughout the summer and fall of 1919. At the peace conference Wilson had told David Lloyd George and others that he thought he could convince Congress to "take a share" in providing large-scale support to the Kolchak government. Realizing that such a campaign would engender controversy, the president refused to take it up before the league question was resolved. In addition, the debilitating series of strokes he suffered in September of that year further immobilized American diplomacy. Despite the prodding of zealous subordinates, Wilson failed to take any initiatives toward the floundering Kolchak regime, beyond increasing the clandestine aid already being given.

It became clear that American antagonism toward the continued military presence in Siberia ran deep even before Wilson returned home. Senator Hiram Johnson, who had criticized the administration's actions in Russia from the start, led the way. On May 20, he introduced a resolution calling upon the executive to justify the intervention and to explain why it was still going on. Five weeks later the Senate unanimously approved Johnson's resolution and forwarded it to the president. Similar resolutions were presented in the House, and ensuing debates revealed formidable opposition to the administration's policy. A number of individuals in both houses (and some members of the press as well) sought to link Russia to the hotly contested league issue. Membership in that organization, they warned, would mean American participation in interventions all over the world at the behest of foreigners sitting in Geneva.

Given these circumstances, it is not surprising that the president refused to take any steps which might aggravate the situation. At a press conference held on July 10, he refused to give any direct answers to questions about Siberia. When asked whether he would express his attitude "toward the Kolchak government or the other governments of Russia," Wilson responded, "No sir. That is an athletic feat, to adjust one's mind to those things."[1] On July 22, he replied to the Johnson resolution in placatory terms. The original reasons for sending American forces, he stated, were to rescue the Czechoslovaks from annihilation by "hostile armies" and to steady Russian efforts at self-defense. Emphasizing the role of organized "enemy prisoners of war" in the struggle, an allegation he had long known to be false, Wilson presented his decision as part of the effort to fight Germany and Austria-Hungary by all possible means. In explaining why American troops had remained in Siberia so long after the armistice, the president shifted to humanitarian grounds. Alluding to the railway agreement with Japan and the functions performed by the Railway Service Corps, he stressed the importance of maintaining the transportation system in Siberia. "The population of Siberia, whose resources have been almost exhausted by the long years of war and the chaotic conditions which have existed there," he said, "can be protected from a further period of chaos and anarchy only by the restoration and maintenance of traffic along the Siberian railway." American troops were there solely for this purpose. Wilson mentioned the Kolchak government once but gave no hint that the United States was supplying that regime with arms and equipment for use in the civil war.[2]

During the latter part of August, the House Committee on

Foreign Affairs held a series of hearings on the subject. Secretary of War Newton D. Baker appeared and, though defending administration policy, he revealed far more than had the president about American relations with the Kolchak government—including the sending of arms and military supplies. Third Assistant Secretary of State Breckenridge Long tried to "correct" the impressions created by Baker. Testifying on August 29 and 31, Long placed American actions in the most favorable light. His version of the original reasons for intervening went beyond the president's. Wilson had cited the threat posed by armies composed of German and Austrian prisoners-of-war; Long asserted that they (along with the Bolsheviks) were in control of the Trans-Siberian railway. Thus, in addition to the plight of the Czechoslovaks, "it was feared that . . . [the] vast stores at Vladivostok would be carried into Germany."[3] Long's statement reinforced the claim that intervention was an act of war against the Central Powers, but it was without factual basis. No government official thought such a danger existed because earlier rumors of prisoner-of-war armies had been untrue.

As to the continued presence of American forces in Siberia, Long elaborated on (and embellished) the president's avowed humanitarianism in guarding and maintaining the transportation system. The arms and munitions forwarded to Kolchak, he insisted, had been sold in legitimate transactions with Russian officials. The third secretary then treated his auditors to a convoluted explanation of why the administration still recognized the Russian embassy which represented no existing government and how the embassy's funds were "absolutely beyond" the administration's control when transactions could be undertaken only with the approval of the State and Treasury Departments. In addition, he defended the propriety of selling goods intended for use in a civil war to a man (Ambassador Bakhmetev) who was "formerly an official of the Kerensky Government, who has close diplomatic or political

119

ties with Mr. Kolchak."* According to Secretary Long, the administration had acted in its belief that "the best interests of civilization would be served with such assistance."

Secretary Long's testimony contained generous portions of half-truths and outright falsehoods and was most notable for what it omitted. As discussed in previous chapters, the United States had assisted Kolchak since his seizure of power in the fall of 1918. The continued recognition of Bakhmetev and the embassy was little more than a cover enabling him to function as Kolchak's procurement officer. Even if the embassy's funds had indeed been "absolutely beyond" the administration's control, which they were not, they properly would have been depleted through paying off debts. The administration had deliberately preserved these assets by deferring its own claims and convincing private bankers to do the same. Then, through devices such as selling goods on the basis of IOUs and miniscule down payments, substantial amounts of "surplus" materials were forwarded to Kolchak at a fraction of their real costs.[4] Long also neglected to inform the committee that the Departments of State and Treasury at that very time were completing negotiations with American and British bankers for a new fifty-million-dollar loan to Kolchak.

During the month preceding Long's testimony, Ambassador Morris's reports from Omsk began arriving in Washington. Morris, it will be recalled, had been sent from his post in Tokyo to evaluate Kolchak's government and to make recommendations about American policies. The ambassador, whose judgments Wilson trusted, reached Omsk late in July and soon began cabling his observations: a sorry tale of inefficiency, ignorance, corruption and, above all, savage repres-

*The last quotation is from the actual transcript of the hearing, a copy of which can be found in Long's papers at the Library of Congress. Permitted to edit the transcript before it was printed as a congressional document, he deleted the word "formerly" and altered the latter part of the statement to read "who is acting in this instance for Admiral Kolchak's Government."

120

sion. "All over Siberia there is an orgy of arrest without charges; of execution without even the pretense of trial; and of confiscation without color of authority."[5] Morris attributed this situation to military elements within Kolchak's Council of Ministers. He felt that Kolchak himself was well meaning but inexperienced, as were his civilian advisers. Their failure to control the military had brought the regime almost to the point of collapse.

Nonetheless, Morris thought he saw some rays of hope amidst the gloom. "Kolchak and his [civilian] colleagues," he stated, "have learned a great deal from the mistakes which they now recognize they have made during the last eight months. The military leaders have lost much of their influence."[6] If Kolchak and others could curb the military, Morris thought, the regime might yet prevent its own demise. Another advantage, the ambassador pointed out, was that moderates in Siberia (whom he thought were in the majority) had only the alternative of Kolchak or bolshevism. Thus a liberalized regime might attract those who had been apathetic at best, actively hostile at worst. And finally, Morris believed that concerted action by Great Britain, France and especially the United States might enable the Omsk government to survive its present crisis and eventually to prevail over the Bolsheviks. Admitting that the regime might collapse no matter what was done to help it, Morris nevertheless advocated assistance, for "we could not be worse off than if we stood by and waited for the event."[7]

The ambassador's specific proposals, as summarized in a memorandum for Secretary Lansing, placed a heavy burden on the administration.[8] First, he recommended that the Kolchak regime be officially recognized as the Provisional Government of Russia, if it survived the present crisis. Second, he suggested advancing $420,000,000 in credits for military and commercial purposes and support of the railways. Finally, he asked that "at least" 25,000 additional American troops replace the Czechoslovaks "who must be withdrawn." Without these reinforcements, Morris warned, the rail lines could not be kept open.

Whether the ambassador actually thought the administration would implement these suggestions is uncertain. If so, he was soon disappointed. On August 25, (just a few days before Secretary Long's evasive testimony before the House committee) Secretary Lansing informed Morris that none of his recommendations would be followed in the near future. No additional American troops could be sent. Neither military nor commercial credits could be created without specific authorization from Congress. "Any action by Congress," Lansing informed the ambassador, "will depend upon whether the President will present plan for assistance which is now being prepared with the help of Mr. [Vance] McCormick on the basis of your reports." The key to that decision was the League of Nations, for "no action by Congress can be urged until the ratification of the Peace Treaty is out of the way." Recognizing the Omsk regime, therefore, was "unfortunately impractical because of the fact that the support which you regard as necessary for Kolchak's success cannot be given."[9]

For whatever consolation it afforded Kolchak, Lansing requested that Morris assure the admiral of the following: shipments of rifles would continue; the War Department was prepared to increase contracts with Siberian cooperative societies from $15,000,000 to $25,000,000; and the release of bank notes (which the United States had printed for Kolchak's use) would follow "conclusion of formalities" for the $50,000,000 loan being negotiated with private bankers. The administration's inability to do more, Morris was to inform the admiral, was "due solely to existing legislation" which tied the president's hands. "Please say to Admiral Kolchak personally," Lansing continued,

> that the inability of this Government to render more
> tangible assistance at this time, while due to facts
> beyond its control is, nevertheless, sincerely regretted

*and must not be construed in any way as suggesting
any lack of appreciation of his own extraordinary
efforts in overcoming great obstacles or of any change
of our hope to assist Russia.*

In short, the Kolchak regime would have to hold on as best it could until the Treaty of Versailles was out of the way.[10]

On September 4, President Wilson began a cross-country speaking tour in behalf of the league. A number of his talks stressed the dangers of bolshevism—"the poison of disorder, the poison of revolt, the poison of chaos"—and warned his listeners that it would spread throughout nations everywhere "so long as the world is kept waiting for the answer of the kind of peace we are going to have." He did not exclude the United States, for "that poison will steadily spread . . . until it may be that even this beloved land of ours will be distracted and distorted by it."[11] At this time, the United States was well into the Red Scare (a period of anti-Communist hysteria immediately following the war) and Wilson clearly was trying to transform the widespread fear of bolshevism into support for the League of Nations.

Kolchak's armies launched their September offensive while the president was away from Washington. Actually little more than a pause in the general retreat, the campaign's limited successes were greatly exaggerated in Consul General Harris's reports from Omsk. On September 19, Assistant Secretary of State William Phillips telegramed Wilson that Kolchak's forces were "driving the Bolsheviki back towards the Urals."[12] Reminding the president that the United States had "joined in undertaking to do its share in supplying Kolchak and his associates with munitions, food, and supplies to the best of its abilities," Phillips urgently recommended that Wilson authorize Secretary of War Baker to sell Ambassador Bakhmetev supplies and equipment on a credit basis. "Our failure to render this assistance," Phillips warned, "will not be understood in Russia and will not only weaken Kolchak but also affect unfavorably our own position to the immediate and possibly permanent advantage of Japan."

Wilson replied the following day. "I fully approve of your proposals," he informed Phillips, ". . . with regard to furnishing such supplies as are available to the forces under Kolchak, and authorize you to show this telegram to the Secretary of Treasury, the Secretary of War, and the Chairman of the Shipping Board." Although the administration had previously used a number of devices to furnish Kolchak with materials, Wilson's decision nullified the restrictions on aid outlined in Secretary Lansing's cable to Morris a month earlier. Whether he would have gone further can never be known.* Five days later Wilson fell ill after completing a speech in Pueblo, Colorado, and the presidential train was ordered back to Washington. Shortly after his arrival, Wilson suffered a severe stroke.

The story of President Wilson's illness can be told only briefly here. After hovering near death for several days, he began to recover but the stroke had paralyzed the left side of his face and body. The precise degree to which he was incapacitated in the weeks following is not known, as Mrs. Wilson and others strove to create the appearance that he was functioning almost normally. They maintained that, though bedridden, the president was alert and fully capable of conducting his administrative duties. This certainly was untrue. Cabinet members were denied access to him and ran their departments as best they could on a day-to-day basis. When presidential decisions were absolutely necessary, officials usually submitted their requests in writing. Replies, when forthcoming, were often only handwritten comments by Mrs. Wilson in the margins of the original letters: "The President

---

*Frank Polk, second-ranking member of the State Department, apparently thought so, as did Assistant Secretary William Phillips. On October 1, Polk noted in his diary that he had told another individual that "as a matter of fact, if it had not been for the President's illness, recognition [of Kolchak] would have been granted." The basis for this assumption is unclear.

desires that . . ." or "the President has decided . . ." No one could be sure which messages Wilson actually had seen or how they were presented to him. In any event, American policy toward Siberia hung in a state of suspension.

During October, information received from Russia caused Secretary of State Lansing to alternate between moods of despair and enthusiasm. He had few illusions about Kolchak's regime—Ambassador Morris's evaluation had punctured earlier ones—and as the September campaign sputtered out, White armies once again began falling back toward Omsk. At the same time, however, anti-Bolshevik forces led by General Anton Denikin launched what appeared to be a major offensive in southern Russia. In the West, Russian and Finnish armies under Generals N. N. Yudenich and Carl Mannerheim reportedly were prepared to move against Petrograd at any moment. Lansing considered these events so promising that he had prepared for Wilson's signature a letter authorizing Ambassador Bakhmetev to purchase 29,000 tons of wheat flour from the United States Grain Corporation for the relief of Petrograd's civilian population after the the city fell.[13] "It is now more probable than at any time in the past that the Bolshevik Government will fall," Lansing stated on October 20. "On this account it is more important than ever that Kolchak be supported."[14]

Such optimism was unwarranted. General Denikin's "drive on Moscow" was blunted and then turned back by Red armies. The more promising Yudenich-Mannerheim offensive never materialized because Kolchak refused to recognize an independent Finland, which the Finns insisted upon as a prerequisite for taking part. "Blinded by national pride and oblivious to the realities of the situation," John M. Thompson has written, "Kolchak refused to yield what the Finns asked, even when his own dreams were in ruins."[15] Omsk fell in mid-November, and the French and British began cutting back on aid to the various White armies. Instead, they concentrated on strengthening states on Russia's western periphery in order to create a *cordon sanitaire* to protect Europe from the spread of bolshevism. Although the fighting continued, intervention had failed and the problem now was how to end the enterprise as gracefully as possible.

In fact, the Americans abandoned intervention without any grace at all. On December 23, Secretary Lansing sent a memorandum to Wilson, recommending that United States troops be withdrawn. "The truth of the matter is the simple fact that the Kolchak Government has utterly collapsed," he wrote:

> The armies of the Bolsheviki have advanced into
> Eastern Siberia, where they are reported to be acting
> with moderation. The people seem to prefer them to
> the officers of the Kolchak regime. Further, the
> Bolshevik army is approaching the region where the
> soldiers are, and contact with them will lead to open
> hostilities and to many complications. In other words,
> if we do not withdraw we shall have to wage war
> against the Bolsheviks. [16]

The bedridden president agreed, and on January 9, 1920, a note was sent to Japan outlining American plans. Unfortunately, because of an error in timing by the War Department, an announcement of the withdrawal was released prematurely in Vladivostok, before Japan received the American message. [17] The Japanese government complained bitterly about not having been consulted but in the end could do little but acknowledge the decision. American participation in the intervention began in confusion and ended the same way.

Ambassador Bakhmetev endeavored to continue the struggle as the Kolchak government neared its end. He proposed that the Americans take the admiral's gold reserve out of Siberia so that the Russian embassy might use it to provision anti-Communist forces in other regions. The State Department turned down his request. When the ambassador pointed out that the administration had "taken sides" all along, he was told that the American government had accepted "the fiction of the Russian Embassy" and sanctioned its aid of Kolchak "hoping that his faction could gather to itself the Russian people and the real Russia could be recognized through him." But "the facts show failure."[18] The United States would do no more than hold the gold reserve in trust until a representative government emerged. The question was academic. Kolchak, knowing his influence depended upon the gold, refused to part with it. By now convinced that the United States had betrayed him, he reportedly declared that he would sooner give it to the Bolsheviks. It turned out that the decision was not his to make.

While the discussions went on in Washington, General Graves in Siberia faced a situation that daily became more explosive. Advancing Red armies, Kolchak's disintegrating government and the unpredictable Cossacks combined to produce chaos along the Trans-Siberian railway east of Omsk. American troops thus far had been able to avoid any large-scale battle, but Colonel Morrow's Twenty-seventh Infantry stationed near Lake Baikal was dangerously exposed. If not evacuated soon, the unit would be engulfed by the tide of humanity moving toward it—compared with which, as one observer put it, Napoleon's retreat seemed a "mere withdrawal."[19]

Kolchak and his entourage left Omsk on the night of November 14.* Travelling east by train, the beleagured admiral left his retreating armies behind, naively thinking he might reestablish his government at Irkutsk. But the situation had deteriorated beyond repair. In Irkutsk, as in other cities along the rail line, Social Revolutionary groups had ousted discredited Kolchak officials. The self-proclaimed "Supreme Ruler of All the Russias" was now helpless, though he continued issuing orders to which no one paid any attention.

---

*As the victorious Red forces entered the city they found warehouses overflowing with food, supplies and equipment. That these materials had not been distributed to the fighting men who needed them was typical of the corrupt and inefficient Kolchak regime.

127

Amidst the masses of troops and civilians streaming along the Trans-Siberian route, only the Czechs maintained discipline. They had their own locomotives, cars and armored trains. Kolchak at first tried to halt the Czech exodus but, at last realizing he had lost any semblance of power, surrendered himself and his gold reserve to the legion for safe passage. The Czechs had no love for the admiral, however, and their sole concern was to reach Vladivostok safely. They took him into custody but were prepared to barter him or the gold for their own protection.

On January 10, 1920, a week after Kolchak had surrendered to the Czechs, American forces again encountered Semenov's troops. Earlier Colonel Morrow had permitted the Cossack leader to send trains through the American sector to suppress the revolt in Irkutsk. On January 9, one of Semenov's armored trains stopped at the Verkhne Udinsk station and a detachment of Cossacks seized the stationmaster. The town of Verkhne Udinsk happened to be where the Twenty-seventh Infantry had established its headquarters, and Colonel Morrow hurried to the station when he learned what had happened. There he informed the train commander, General N. Bogomoletz, that there would be no such arrests in the American sector of the rail line.[20] Bogomoletz replied that Morrow had no jurisdiction in the matter and that the conversation was over. "I informed General Bogomoletz that the conversation was just beginning," Morrow later recalled, "and if he did not release the stationmaster, I would forcibly take him away with American troops." The Russian relented, and the incident seemed closed as the armored train left Verkhne Udinsk, heading west.

About sixty miles up the line a detachment of forty Americans was quartered in boxcars at the Posolskaya station. Later that evening the Russian armored train steamed into Posolskaya. For a time there was no discernible movement on the train. Then, a little after midnight, its gunports opened and the Cossacks began firing at the boxcars. This was not, however, a repetition of the Romanovka massacre. Sentries had alerted the Americans when the train pulled in, and now they poured out of the boxcars, firing and throwing grenades at every aperture. Running alongside the train under the gunports, the soldiers rendered useless the cannon and machine guns. Sgt. Carl Robbins reached the locomotive and threw a grenade into the cab—he was killed almost instantly.

General Bogomoletz, realizing he had gotten into more than he could handle, gave orders to move out of danger. At first the train picked up speed, leaving the Americans behind. But since grenades had pierced the boilers in a number of places, the locomotive wheezed to a stop and the Cossacks were stranded. Fearing local guerrilla forces more than the Americans, Bogomoletz sent back word that he wished to surrender to the detachment at Posolskaya. "I am sorry that Lieutenant Kendall [officer in charge of the men at the station], who first got hold of Bogomoletz, did not hang him to a telegraph pole," General Graves wrote of the incident, but he concluded that the young officer had behaved correctly. Semenov demanded the return of Bogomoletz and his troops, claiming they would be punished appropriately. Colonel Morrow imprisoned them for a while but with great reluctance later turned them over.* Two weeks after the Posolskaya incident Graves ordered the Twenty-seventh to begin the long journey back to Vladivostok.

Admiral Kolchak was not so fortunate. The Czechs, who had him in custody, were fighting a rear guard action against the Bolsheviks as they moved eastward. The legion was prepared to fight its way out if necessary, but Kolchak and his gold reserve provided bargaining leverage. Using the Irkutsk Social Revolutionaries as intermediaries, the Czechs offered

---

*Bogomoletz later made his way to the United States and worked as a shoemaker in Hollywood until 1938. At that time he was deported on the grounds of moral turpitude because he had misrepresented his marital status when he applied for American citizenship!

to deliver both to the Reds in return for an armistice permitting the legion to evacuate without hindrance. The Bolsheviks accepted. Kolchak was abandoned to the Social Revolutionaries, who in turn were soon displaced by the Bolsheviks. The admiral was tried by a Soviet court in Irkutsk and executed by a firing squad on February 7, 1920.[21] The gold was sent to Moscow.

The Departments of War and State clashed to the very end. Upon General Graves's recommendation, Secretary Baker ordered the consolidation of all American forces at Vladivostok as quickly as possible. The State Department protested. Acting Secretary Polk informed Baker that reports from Siberia indicated that the Czech evacuation would be impeded, if not actually endangered, should the Americans abandon their sectors. Baker's reply was less than cordial. Given the fact that there were some 65,000 Czech troops along the rail lines, compared with approximately 5,000 Americans, it was far more likely that the legion would afford protection for the Americans rather than the reverse. Polk did not pursue his objections.[22]

The exodus of Czechs and Americans proceeded without any major incidents, though the Japanese and the Cossacks proved less than cooperative. Semenov's control over the region around Chita was crumbling; there had been mutinies and desertions. Partisan bands, some of them Red, some merely anti-Kolchak or anti-Semenov, took over the abandoned sectors. "Our relations with the Partisans had improved," one veteran of the A.E.F. in Siberia has written, "until they were now very different from what they had been during the previous spring and summer."[23] At some villages delegations of peasants visited the Americans, wishing them well and exchanging gifts.

The city of Vladivostok, already swollen far beyond its prewar population was now inundated by the arriving Czech and American troops. Local Social Revolutionaries had overthrown the last vestige of Kolchak's government by the end of

January, but there was no friction with the Americans. Indeed, the new government worked smoothly with Graves in preventing any civil disturbances through a very trying period. During the last few months he spent in Vladivostok, Graves recalled, "I never saw anyone try harder to be fair and just to everyone than did these people."[24]

The embarkation was routine: loading equipment, delousing the men, preparing the rosters. There was one exception. Some of the soldiers had established more than casual relationships with Russian women. Chaplain Joseph S. Loughran performed about eighty marriages during the last few weeks in Vladivostok and was assigned to accompany the new brides on one of the transports bound for Manila. The American departures continued through March, and on April 1, 1920, headquarters and the last units cleared port. After almost two years, the Siberian intervention was over—for the Americans at least. As the troops sailed away, one veteran wrote, "there was no cheering and little to be said."[25]

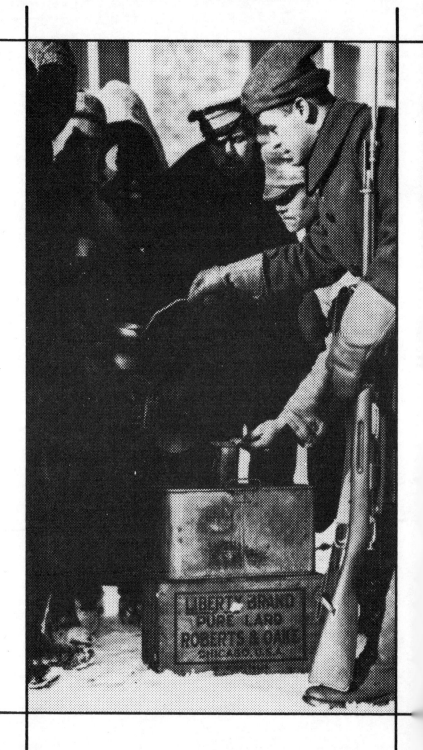

An Overview

8

The Siberian intervention continued after American and Czechoslovakian troops departed. The Japanese contingent stayed on until late 1922, when domestic opposition and steady diplomatic pressure from the Western nations forced the military into a reluctant withdrawal. An organization calling itself the Far Eastern Republic had arisen in Vladivostok following Kolchak's demise, but it was short-lived, abolishing itself shortly after the Japanese left and eastern Siberia became an "integral part" of Soviet Russia. By this time, Woodrow Wilson was out of office, an embittered invalid denouncing the evil men who had thwarted his plans for creating a peaceful world.

Historians agree that Wilson's reasons for participating in the intervention were more complex than he stated publicly. The most common interpretation emphasizes his wish to check Japanese expansion: convinced that Japan meant to establish hegemony over eastern Siberia if it went in alone, he sought to frustrate its ambitions by interposing American forces. According to this view, Wilson was merely trying to preserve an "open door" until the Russians themselves could reassert control. Other scholars see intervention as primarily an anti-Bolshevik measure. With the ultimate goal of unseating the Moscow regime, blocking the Japanese was an important but subsidiary task. Since the administration never seriously considered working with the Soviets, it is argued, their overthrow constituted the basis for an open door regardless of Japanese intentions.

The burden of proof necessary to uphold the latter interpretation has been a heavy one. Thus far scholars have relied mostly upon Wilson's frequently expressed hope that a Russian "strongman" would depose the Communists and the

135

efforts of the Western Allies and certain members of the State Department to turn intervention into a crusade against bolshevism. Certainly, the president detested communism and hoped for a successful counterrevolution, but this does not prove he tried to promote one. As for the sentiments of the European powers and State Department officials, Wilson rarely allowed such considerations to deflect him once he had decided upon a course of action. While his public statements, his insistence on neutral conduct by American forces in Siberia and his behavior at the Paris Peace Conference lend substance to the thesis that he did not wish to interfere in Russia's domestic affairs, that thesis is incorrect. In fact, he intended to prevent the establishment of bolshevism in Russia if he could, and intervention was one means.

Several factors caused Wilson to conceal his real goals. Keenly aware that open participation in the Russian civil war might actually strengthen the Bolsheviks, he refused to act until the plight of the Czechs provided "the shadow of a plan" which he thought might avoid the stigma of interference. In addition, the president distrusted French and British motives. Until the tide of war turned in the West, he feared their consuming desire for a second front rendered them untrustworthy as partners in Siberia. All along, he had grave misgivings about what kind of Russia they wanted to emerge. He was suspicious of Japanese ambitions too; but they could act independently, so he tried to bind them to a program of his own devising. Finally, American domestic politics led Wilson to move cautiously and, at times, deceptively. Opposition to getting entangled in Russia was widespread and might threaten membership in the League of Nations which he regarded as vital for world peace.

Wilson had available to him several ploys which appeared acceptable and remained comparatively safe from congressional assault. His use of them permits small doubt that he intended to and did interfere in Russia as much as possible within the limits imposed upon him. Authorized under the

Liberty Loan Act of 1917 to extend loans without the specific approval of Congress to nations engaged in war against the Central Powers, he underwrote British- and French-sponsored campaigns against the Bolsheviks within weeks of the November Revolution. He allocated ten million dollars of his own war fund for use in Siberia, a considerable portion of which went for aid to the White armies. The United States participated unofficially but actively in a blockade designed to starve out Communist-held regions and manipulated relief programs to the same end. Finally, the administration's clandestine use of the Russian embassy's resources shows Wilson's deep commitment to the anti-Bolshevik cause. As Ambassador Bakhmetev said later, Wilson ignored his "liberal" friends who urged him to reach an agreement with the Soviet government; instead he tried to destroy it.[1]

If this interpretation is correct, intervention must be judged a total failure.* Whether any action the United States might have taken, short of a full-scale invasion, would have significantly altered events is conjectural. As it was, the immediate effect of intervention was to prolong a bloody civil war, thereby costing thousands of additional lives and wreaking enormous destruction on an already battered society. And there were longer-range implications. Bolshevik leaders had clear proof, if they needed any, that the Western powers meant to destroy the Soviet government if given the chance. Some scholars have accepted at face value Cordell Hull's naive assertion that, as secretary of state in 1933, he convinced Soviet negotiators of America's good intentions by showing them a selection of documents from the earlier period. The Russians knew better: they had obtained their own

---

*Those who stress Wilson's desire to contain the Japanese argue that American participation partially achieved this goal. It is difficult to see how. The Japanese acted without restraint while the Americans were there, and remained alone for more than two and one-half years. The factors which eventually caused Japan to withdraw would have obtained regardless of the A.E.F.'s presence between 1918 and 1920.

collection of letters and cables when they captured Admiral Kolchak's records. The extent to which the memory of intervention influenced Josef Stalin's conduct during the 1930s and '40s cannot be known—he alluded to it several times during World War II conferences—but it must have deepened the suspicions of a congenitally suspicious man.

How could the president have embarked upon a venture which, in retrospect, had so little chance of success? His fundamental error lay in his assumptions about the democratic instincts of the Russian people. Wilson was inclined to believe that he knew what other peoples wanted, which somehow always coincided with what he wanted for them. In his view, the Bolsheviks were interlopers who had seized power during a period of turmoil, and they no more represented the "real" Russia than did the tsar. The Bolsheviks themselves Wilson regarded as fanatical believers in unrealistic social and economic doctrines. This outlook caused him to underestimate the ability of the Soviets to sustain and consolidate their power, and at the same time to exaggerate the prospects for rallying a war-weary people to yet another crusade.

Wilson never believed the task would be an easy one. Neither the Directory nor the Kolchak government provided inspirational leadership, and the latter regime stoutly refused to reform itself despite Wilson's efforts. Yet the attempt had to be made because the stakes were so high. Just as he had concluded that the kaiser's government must be destroyed to secure lasting peace, so Wilson could not abide a Bolshevik tyranny. Indeed, when it appeared that bolshevism might spread into Eastern and Central Europe, Wilson felt it became all the more important to eradicate the contagion at its source. The president acted not because of the relatively minor issue of an Open Door in Siberia, but because he wanted to create an enduring postwar world.

Notes

For the purpose of brevity, the notes listed below have been restricted to direct quotations and to materials not readily available in the secondary works cited in the bibliography.

Introduction

1. *Foreign Relations of the United States*, 1917, Supplement I, *The World War* (1931), 200. Hereafter cited as *FRUS*.
2. The materials leading up to and including the Passport Questions are from the author's "The American Jewish Committee and the Passport Question," master's thesis, University of Wisconsin, 1958.

Chapter 1

1. House to Wilson, July 19, 1917, Woodrow Wilson Papers, Series II.
2. *New York Times*, July 27, 1917; *Current History* 21 (September, 1917), 465-66.
3. Lincoln Steffens, *Autobiography*, 770-72; Edith Bolling Wilson, *My Memoir*, 138.
4. Ray Stannard Baker, *Woodrow Wilson: Life and Letters*, 6:204.
5. *FRUS*, 1918, *Russia*, 1:218.
6. *New York Times*, November 9 and 10, 1917.
7. *Ibid.*, November 10, 1917.
8. Baker, 6:355.

Chapter 2

1. Jane Degras, ed., *Soviet Documents on Foreign Policy*, 1:1.
2. *New York Times*, November 13, 1917.
3. *Ibid.*, December 5, 1917.
4. *The Fourteen Points*, House Document.
5. The most detailed published summary of the Russian embassy's financial situation is *Loans to Foreign Governments*, Senate Document.
6. Transcript of oral recording, Boris Bakhmetev, Oral History Project, Columbia University Library. Hereafter cited as Bakhmetev, *Transcript*.
7. *New York Times*, November 11, 1917.
8. *Ibid.*, November 25, December 14, 1917.
9. For details of arrangements between Bakhmetev and American agencies, see International Fiscal Relationships, Record Group 39, "Country File," Box 199, National Archives. Hereafter cited as "Country File." See also Frank Polk Diary, November 10, 26 and 30, 1917, Polk Papers.
10. David Lloyd George, *War Memoirs*, 5:114.
11. *FRUS*, 1918, *Russia* (1932), 2:582.
12. Lansing memorandum, December 10, 1917, Wilson Papers, Series 2.
13. Lansing Desk Diary, December 10, 11, 12, 13 and 17, 1917, Robert Lansing Papers.
14. State Department Records, 861.00/804D, December 12, 1917, National Archives. Hereafter cited by file number only.
15. For Wilson's temporary acquiescence and subsequent retreat, see House to Wilson, March 3, 1918, Edward M. House Papers. At the top of his own copy, House wrote, "After the President received this he recalled from the State Dept. the note that was to have been sent to Japan." See also Polk Diary, March 4, 1918.
16. Wilson to Lansing, March 22, 1918, 861.00/433½.
17. Sir William Wiseman to Eric Drummond, March 14, 1918, Sir William Wiseman Papers.
18. Wilson to Lansing, April 18, 1918, 861.00/1602½.
19. *Ibid.*, undated, attached to correspondence of late May, 861.00/1895½.
20. Wiseman to Drummond, May 30, 1918, Wiseman Papers.

140

Chapter 3

1. "Welcome as the American reinforcements are," London cabled Wiseman on July 3, 1918, "their value in resisting constantly increasing anarchy in Russia enables Germans to transfer divisions to the west." Arthur Murray to Wiseman, Wiseman Papers.
2. Baker, 7:284.
3. Wilson to Lansing, June 17, 1918, 861.00/2145½.
4. *Ibid.* On June 24, Lansing asked Third Assistant Secretary Breckenridge Long to determine the "availability of guns and ammunition made for Russians now in U.S. and England." Long Diary, Breckenridge Long Papers, Library of Congress.
5. House Diary, July 9, 1918.
6. See "Memorandum of a Conference at the White House in Reference to the Siberian Situation," July 6, 1918, 861.00/2240½.
7. For Wilson's conversation with the British ambassador, see Lord Reading to Foreign Office, July 8, 1918, Wiseman Papers. See also House Diary, July 9. Alluding to Wilson's desire to bind Japan to his program, House wrote, "When he does this, he will undoubtedly advise the other powers, but until then, he considers it unnecessary."
8. *FRUS, The Lansing Papers, 1914-1920*, 2:372-73.
9. For British and French protests, see Lansing to Wilson, July 9, Polk Papers, and Lord Reading to Prime Minister and Mr. Balfour, July 9, Wiseman Papers.
10. Japan's reply to Wilson's proposal is attached to letter, Polk to Lansing, July 24, 1918, 861.00/2358½. See also Polk Diary, July 24, for his interview with Japanese ambassador.
11. Wilson's aide-mémoire is printed in *FRUS*, 1918, *Russia*, 2:287-90.
12. See Lansing to Wilson, May 16, 1918, 861.00/1894½.
13. House Diary, July 25, 1918.
14. Alvey Adee memorandum to William Phillips, June 28, 1918, 861.00/2133.
15. See Vance McCormick to Gen. Peyton C. March, October 30, and March to McCormick, October 31, 1918, unnumbered

box, Records of Executive Office, War Trade Board, National Archives.
16. William S. Graves, *America's Siberian Adventure*, 4.

Chapter 4

1. Graves, 56.
2. *Ibid.*, 76.
3. John Bradley, *Allied Intervention in Russia*, 107-10.
4. For information on Kolchak, see Charles J. Weeks, Jr., and Joseph O. Baylen, "Admiral Kolchak's Mission to the United States, 10 September-9 November, 1917," *Military Affairs* 40, No. 2 (April 1976), 63-67.
5. See Lansing Desk Diary, August 23 and 26, 1918, and Bahkmetev, *Transcript*.
6. Graves, 126.
7. Although he seems not to have joined the intrigue against Graves, Lansing originally recommended against his appointment. Graves, Lansing wrote, "has not the tact and diplomacy which is required to deal with so delicate a situation." July 31, 1918, Polk Papers.
8. Graves, 160.
9. This quotation and the preceding account of the clash with Semenov is from "The American Expeditionary Force in Siberia as a Part of Allied Intervention in 1918," a paper read by Lieutenant Colonel H. H. Slaughter at the Army War College, March 29, 1934. Copy on file at the War College, Carlisle, Pennsylvania.
10. Graves, 354.

Chapter 5

1. George F. Kennan, *Russia Leaves the War*, 446.
2. House Diary, September 24, 1918.
3. Notes of an interview with Wilson by Sir William Wiseman, October 16, 1918, Wiseman Papers.
4. Baker, 7:553.

5. See *FRUS*, 1919, *Russia*, 515-26.

6. *Loans to Foreign Governments*, 116.

7. Captain Hurban to American Consul, Vladivostok, October 28, 1918, War Trade Board, Records of Executive Office.

8. Vance McCormick to Gen. Peyton C. March, October 30, 1918, War Trade Board, Records of the Executive Office.

9. Wilson to Lansing, September 12, 1918, Wilson Papers, Series 3, Letterbook 55.

10. Johnson to Raymond Robins, Box 14, Robins Papers, Wisconsin Historical Society.

11. Herbert Hoover, *The Ordeal of Woodrow Wilson*, 115-16.

12. For the full text of the Prinkipo proposal, see Department of State, *Paris Peace Conference*, 3:676-77.

13. John M. Thompson, *Russia, Bolshevism, and the Versailles Peace*, 117-19.

14. For Bullitt's report to Wilson, see Bullitt to Wilson, March 16, 1919, Wilson Papers, Series 5B. Bullitt concluded that "there is no doubt whatever of the desire of the Soviet Government for a just and reasonable peace, or of the sincerity of this proposal, and I pray you will consider it with the deepest seriousness."

15. Lansing to Polk, January 27, 1919, 861.00/3724. The secretary told several State Department officials that calling the Prinkipo conference "was just one of those things that you kind of had to do but it really wasn't intended." Transcript of oral recording, DeWitt C. Poole, Oral History Project, Columbia University Library.

16. *FRUS*, 1919, *Russia*, 57-59.

17. For the exchange of cables with Polk, see *FRUS*, 1919, *Russia*, 243-51.

18. By April 29, 1919, Wilson was considering provisional recognition of Kolchak "in view of the success attending the arms of the Omsk Government during the past month."

19. For the Allied note of May 26, see *FRUS*, 1919, *Russia*, 367-70. Earlier, on May 17, Wilson had sent a unilateral message to Kolchak indicating that the United States would be more favorably inclined toward recognition provided Kolchak agreed to certain reforms. Wilson to Vance McCormick, May 16, 1919, Wilson Papers, Series 5B.

20. For the exchange between David Lloyd George and Wilson over getting Congress to "take a share," see *FRUS*, 1919, *Russia*, 363, 386.
21. Basil Miles to Lansing, May 21, and Lansing to State Department, May 26, 1919, *Loans to Foreign Governments*, 142-43, 146.

Chapter 6

1. Polk to Lansing, April 17, 1919, Polk Papers.
2. Graves and Baker quotations are in messages transmitted by Gen. Tasker Bliss to Wilson, May 9, 1919, Wilson Papers, Series 8A.
3. See Graves to Adjutant General, May 17, 1919, Office of the Adjutant General, Project Files, 1917, 1925, National Archives.
4. Graves, 85-86.
5. For Baker's defense of Graves, see Baker to Wilson, March 18, 1919, Wilson Papers, Series 5B, and Baker to Wilson, May 21, copied verbatim in Gordon Auchincloss Diary, Auchincloss Papers, Yale University Library.
6. Account of the Romanovka Massacre constructed from reminiscences of veterans of the A.E.F., Siberia, collected by Joseph Longuevan, deposited at the Army War College, Carlisle, Pennsylvania. The songs following are from the same source.
7. Graves to Adjutant General, May 17, 1919, Office of the Adjutant General, Project Files, 1917-1925.
8. Graves, 216.
9. Morris to Secretary of State, August 4, 1919, Newton D. Baker Papers, Library of Congress.
10. Polk to American Embassy, Tokyo, May 21, 1919, 861.00/4090a.
11. Graves, 228-34.
12. *Ibid.*, 236-37.
13. *FRUS*, 1919, *Russia*, 521.
14. Phillips to Polk, September 26, 1919, Polk Papers.
15. Long Diary, September 24, 1919.

144

16. For the possible repercussions of recalling Graves after the beating, see Bakhmetev, *Transcript*. Bakhmetev recalled a very agitated State Department official telling him, "Can you imagine what will happen if the press should get hold of this— or if Congress should get hold of it?" He went on to say that the incident made recalling Graves "out of the question."
17. Baker to Graves, September 26, 1919, Long Papers.
18. R. Ernest Dupuy, *Perish by the Sword*, 241.
19. Graves, 290-91.
20. *Ibid.*, 282.

Chapter 7

1. July 10, 1919, Wilson Papers, Series 2.
2. Wilson quotations are from "President's Response to Senate Resolution as to the Reasons for Retaining American Troops in Siberia," copy in Long Papers, Box 187.
3. All quotations from Long's testimony can be found in the above source.
4. Each month Bakhmetev submitted to the Treasury Department a form letter stating that "I formally undertake on behalf of the Provisional Government of Russia . . . to pay. . . ." See "Country File," Box 176.
5. Morris to Lansing, July 27, 1919, Long Papers.
6. *Ibid.*, August 4, 1919, Long Papers.
7. *Ibid.*, August 6, 1919, Long Papers.
8. Memorandum for the secretary of state, August 14, 1919, Long Papers.
9. Lansing to Morris, August 25, 1919, Long Papers.
10. *Ibid.*
11. Phillips to American Mission, Copenhagen, September 10, 1919, 861.00/5168.
12. Exchange between Phillips and Wilson, September 19 and 20, 1919, Wilson Papers, Series 4.
13. For Wilson's approval of wheat sale, see Lansing to Wilson and Wilson to president of U.S. Grain Corporation, both October 22, 1919, Wilson Papers, Series 4.

14. Lansing to American Mission, Paris, October 11, 1919, 861.00/5428.

15. Thompson, 333.

16. Lansing to Wilson, December 23, 1919, 861.00/6107.

17. For explanation of how the decision to withdraw became public prematurely, see Division of Russian Affairs memorandum to Lansing, January 9, 1920, 861.00/6126.

18. Exchange between Bakhmetev and State Department officials is in *Loans to Foreign Governments*, 172-73. See also Bakhmetev to Long, January 27, 1919, Long Papers.

19. Sylvian G. Kindall, *American Soldiers in Siberia*, 246.

20. Accounts of Bogomoletz affair are in Dupuy, 260-65, and Graves, 311-13.

21. For Kolchak's trial, see Elena Varneck and H. H. Fisher, eds., *The Testimony of Kolchak and Other Siberian Materials*.

22. For the Polk-Baker exchange, see *FRUS*, 1920, 3:498-504.

23. Kindall, 248.

24. Graves, 324.

25. Kindall, 251.

Overview

1. Bakhmetev, *Transcript*.

Selected Bibliography

MANUSCRIPTS

Army War College, Carlisle, Pennsylvania
Joseph Longuevan Papers

Butler Library, Columbia University
Oral History Research Office: transcripts of reminiscences of
  Boris Bakhmetev, DeWitt C. Poole and Thomas D. Thacher.

Firestone Library, Princeton University
Bernard Baruch Papers
Arthur Bullard Papers

Library of Congress
Newton D. Baker Papers
Tasker H. Bliss Papers
William E. Borah Papers
Norman H. Davis Papers
Hermann Hagedorn-William Boyce Thompson Papers
Robert Lansing Papers
Breckenridge Long Papers
John Bassett Moore Papers
Roland S. Morris Papers
Woodrow Wilson Papers

State Historical Society of Wisconsin, University of Wisconsin

Alexander Gumberg Papers
DeWitt C. Poole Papers
Raymond Robins Papers

Sterling Library, Yale University

Gordon Auchincloss Papers
William C. Bullitt Papers
Edward M. House Papers
Vance D. McCormick Papers
Frank Polk Papers
Sir William Wiseman Papers

UNPUBLISHED DOCUMENTS, NATIONAL ARCHIVES

Department of State, Decimal Files
International Fiscal Relationships (Record Group 39),
    "Country Files"
Records of the Adjutant General's Office, Project Files 1917-1919
Records of the American Commission to Negotiate Peace
War Trade Board, Records of Executive Office
World War I Records of the Supreme War Council,
    War Department

PUBLISHED DOCUMENTS

Official

United States Department of State, *Papers Relating to the Foreign
    Relations of the United States*:

   The Lansing Papers, 1914-1920 (2 vols.; Washington, 1939-1940)
   1917, *Supplement 2*, Vol. 1 (Washington, 1932)
   1918, *Russia* (3 vols.; Washington, 1931-1932)
   1919, *Russia* (Washington, 1937)
   Paris Peace Conference (13 vols.; Washington, 1942-1947)

United States House of Representatives Document 765, *The Fourteen Points*, 65th Congress, 2nd Session.

United States Senate Document 61, *Brewing and Liquor Interests and German and Bolshevik Propaganda*, 66th Congress, 1st Session.

United States Senate Document 172, *Memorandum on Certain Aspects of the Bolshevik Movement in Russia*, 66th Congress, 2nd Session.

United States Senate Documents, *Loans to Foreign Governments*, 67th Congress, 2nd Session.

Unofficial

Bunyan, James. *Intervention, Civil War, and Communism in Russia April-December 1918* (Baltimore, 1936)

Cumming, C. K. and W. W. Pettit. *Russian-American Relations, March 1917-March 1920, Documents and Papers* (New York, 1920)

Degras, Jane. *Soviet Documents on Foreign Policy* (3 vols.; London, 1951-1953)

Varneck, Elena and H. H. Fisher. *The Testimony of Kolchak and Other Siberian Materials* (Stanford, 1935)

LETTERS, MEMOIRS, ETC.

Baker, Ray Stannard. *Woodrow Wilson: Life and Letters* (Potomac Edition. 7 vols.; New York, 1946)

Graves, William S. *America's Siberian Adventure, 1918-1920* (New York, 1931)

Hoover, Herbert. *The Ordeal of Woodrow Wilson* (New York, 1958)

Kindall, Sylvian G. *American Soldiers in Siberia* (New York, 1945)

Lansing, Robert. *The Peace Negotiations: A Personal Narrative* (Boston, 1921)

————. *War Memoirs* (Indianapolis, 1935)

THE UNKNOWN WAR WITH RUSSIA

Lloyd George, David. *Memoirs of the Peace Conference* (2 vols.; New Haven, 1939)

————. *War Memoirs* (6 vols.; Boston, 1933-1937)

March, Peyton C. *The Nation at War* (Garden City, 1932)

Masaryk, Thomas G. *The Making of a State* (New York, 1927)

Seymour, Charles. *The Intimate Papers of Colonel House* (4 vols.; Boston, 1926-1928)

Steffens, Lincoln. *Autobiography* (2 vols.; New York, 1931)

Ward, John. *With the Die-Hards in Siberia* (London, 1920)

Wilson, Edith Bolling. *My Memoir* (Bridgeport, 1938)

ARTICLES

Fike, Claude E. "The Influence of the Creel Committee and the American Red Cross on Russian-American Relations, 1917-1919," *The Journal of Modern History* 31 (June 1959), 93-109

————. "The United States and Russian Territorial Problems, 1917-1920," *Historian* 24 (May 1962), 331-46

Kennan, George F. "The Sisson Documents," *Journal of Modern History* 28 (June 1956), 130-54

Lasch, Christopher. "American Intervention in Siberia: A Reinterpretation," *Political Science Quarterly* 77 (June 1962), 205-23

Maddox, Robert James. "Woodrow Wilson, the Russian Embassy and Siberian Intervention," *Pacific Historical Review* 36 (November 1967), 435-48

Weeks, Charles J., Jr., and Joseph O. Baylen. "Admiral Kolchak's Mission to the United States, 10 September-9 November, 1917," *Military Affairs* 40 (April 1976), 63-67

Williams, William Appleman. "American Intervention in Russia, 1917-1920," *Studies on the Left* 3 (1963), 24-48, and 4 (1964), 39-57

150

BOOKS

Bradley, John. *Allied Intervention in Russia* (New York, 1968)

Dupuy, R. Ernest. *Perish By the Sword* (Harrisburg, 1939)

Fischer, Louis. *The Soviets in World Affairs: A History of Relations Between the Soviet Union and the Rest of the World* (2 vols.; London, 1930)

Kennan, George F. *Russia and the West Under Lenin and Stalin* (Boston, 1961)

————. *Russia Leaves the War* (Princeton, 1956)

————. *The Decision to Intervene* (Princeton, 1958)

Lasch, Christopher. *The American Liberals and the Russian Revolution* (New York, 1962)

Levin, N. Gordon, Jr. *Woodrow Wilson and World Politics: America's Response to War and Revolution* (New York, 1968)

Mayer, Arno J. *Political Origins of the New Diplomacy* (New Haven, 1959)

————. *Policy and Diplomacy of Peacemaking: Containment and Counterrevolution at Versailles, 1918-1919* (New York, 1967)

Morley, James W. *The Japanese Thrust into Siberia, 1918* (New York, 1957)

Thompson, John M. *Russia, Bolshevism, and the Versailles Peace* (Princeton, 1966)

Tillman, Seth P. *Anglo-American Relations at the Paris Peace Conference of 1919* (Princeton, 1961)

Tompkins, Pauline. *American-Russian Relations in the Far East* (New York, 1949)

Ullman, Richard H. *Anglo-Soviet Relations, 1917-1921*, Volume I: *Intervention and the War* (Princeton, 1961)

Unterberger, Betty Miller. *America's Siberian Expedition, 1918-1920* (Durham, 1956)

White, John A. *The Siberian Intervention* (Princeton, 1950)

Index

153